Doors of Opportunity

Conversations with the Revd Marjorie Maltby

Compiled by Erica Taylor

Marjorie Maltby

Published by
Erica Taylor, 93 Welholme Avenue, Grimsby,
North East Lincolnshire DN32 0BP
2004

ISBN: 0 9548636 0 7

Erica Taylor first met Marjorie Maltby at North Hykeham in 1963 when training to be a Local Preacher, and is now a tutor herself. She taught for 23 years at the Stanford School in Laceby and researched its history for her MA. She also wrote a textbook for primary schools.

Printed by
F W Cupit (Printers) Ltd, The Ropewalk, 23 Louth Road,
Horncastle, Lincolnshire LN9 5ED

Marjorie in her Deaconess uniform, Liverpool 1950.

Acknowledgements

Many hours of entertaining conversation and laughter preceded this book so first of all thanks must be given to Marjorie Maltby herself for giving time, energy and thought to identifying and recording her doors of opportunity.

Considerable thanks are due to Sally, Brian and Simon Shuel for producing the first draft and for their considerable encouragement.

Thanks must also go to all those far and wide who read the first draft and sent back their comments and advice. This was invaluable. Particular mention should be made of Shirley and Arnold Tucker who did proof reading at this stage.

It is with great pleasure that thanks go to John Mitchell for his foreword because of his crucial role in Newcastle.

Very grateful thanks go to Ann White for detailed proof-reading and suggestions with the final draft.

A very considerable debt of gratitude is due to David Robinson who has given instintingly of his time and experience in editing and designing this book.

Last but not least, my personal thanks go to my husband and family for their patience, support and considerable advice throughout this time.

Contents

Foreword

I am glad Marjorie Maltby has been persuaded to write this book of personal memoirs. It is a most interesting story and the testimony of one who has served on the frontiers of the church's ministry and missionary activity. It is an honour to have been asked to contribute a Foreword to this book.

The name of Marjorie Maltby was known to me before I ever met her. At the time she was engaged in Industrial Chaplaincy work in Manchester. In this ministry, as in other situations, she was often the sole representative of the Church, and greatly respected. When she came to Newcastle upon Tyne to become a colleague she was a long-standing and valued member of the Wesley Deaconess Order. She was content and fulfilled in the Order but her Call was to a ministry long since denied to women in Methodism.

Marjorie came to Newcastle to continue the work of Methodist International House in a way very different from the traditional provision of a home for students which by that time had become redundant to students' needs. With the proceeds of sale from the M I H in Jesmond an office suite in the city centre became the base for a ministry of pastoral care, counselling, learning and hospitality. Marjorie excelled in what was again a pioneering ministry. She became a friend, much loved, not just in the Newcastle District but across the world in those countries to which 'her students' returned on the completion of their studies.

Marjorie's arrival in Newcastle came at a great historical moment in the life of the Methodist Church. The door was opening to the ordination of women to the Ministry of Word and Sacraments, the opportunity for which many women in Methodism had waited long. The chance for Marjorie to candidate – but only just. A further delay of one year even in the Conference's historic decision would probably have prevented her from proceeding because of age. Even so there were obstacles in the way, thankfully to be overcome. One senior colleague was reluctant to give her his support because he thought she could make a greater contribution to the Deaconess Order. Where support and sponsorship was essential there was opposition to women candidates. At this crucial and critical stage a bold decision was required and Marjorie and I became colleagues and friends. It was a great privilege for me to have some part in promoting and supporting Marjorie during this period of her ministry. The Methodist Conference in Bristol in 1974 was a memorable occasion. Marjorie was one of the first women to be ordained to the Ministry of Word and Sacrament in Methodism. I was honoured to be one of those who laid hands on the head of this acceptable and gifted ordinand.

Marjorie's story tells of the way God calls his servants to ministry and the variety of ways in which He uses them. It illustrates the faithfulness of those who are called and are not diverted from the chosen path when face to face with obstacles and personal sorrow. A story that is unfinished. Marjorie's experience and gifts continue to be used in retirement.

John Mitchell

Introduction

"Take the controls, Marjorie..... Now, bank gently to the left..... Level out."

I stared down in wonderment as we circled the Humber Bridge, flew back over an opencast chalk quarry and lined up for the runway.

"Very good. I'll take over now," said the pilot. We landed and taxied to the apron.

This 'taster' flying lesson had been one of Marjorie's 80th birthday presents!

Revd Marjorie Maltby can often be seen striding along the streets in the shadow of Lincoln Cathedral wearing a red jacket, face to the wind. In early December this part of Lincoln is host to the Christmas Market which attracts visitors from all over Britain, the continent of Europe and the USA. Bailgate Methodist Church, just inside the Roman Newport Arch, opens its doors at that time and members offer rest, hospitality and endless refreshments. There is a list of helpers and a rota of duties. Marjorie chats and circulates, welcoming those who come in. On the rota she also appears as a 'runner.'!

Harry and I were living with our three children in North Hykeham when Marjorie was given charge of Moor Lane and Hykeham Village Methodist Churches in 1963. Harry took up a post on the Humber Bank in 1964, but such was the quality of Marjorie's ministry that we have continued to keep in touch ever since. On one occasion when she came to Weelsby Road Methodist Church, Grimsby, the writer of the notice sheet described our preacher as 'the truly remarkable Marjorie Maltby.' Those who know Marjorie would not have been in the least surprised.

Marjorie believes that in her life she has been given doors of opportunity to pass through in order to fulfil her calling. Conversations with her have afforded glimpses through those varied and fascinating doors of opportunity.

Naturally, as she reminisced, she remembered the advice given by Lewis Carroll: 'Begin at the beginning and go on till you come to the end: then stop.'

This recorded account may have come to an end, but for Marjorie Maltby doors of opportunity continue to open with every passing day.　　　　Thanks be to God.

Erica Taylor

Marjorie climbs aboard for her 80th birthday flying lesson.

Marjorie's mother Lucy with her brother Fred as a baby.

The thatched house at Sotby of Marjorie's paternal grandfather John.

Early Years
1911 to early 1920s

I WAS born on 9th September 1911 at Sotby, between Horncastle and Wragby, in the county of Lincolnshire. My mother was the daughter of a local farmer near Louth. She had five sisters. Amy was the eldest, Matilda, Harriet and Charlotte came before Lucy, my mother, and Rebecca was the youngest daughter. She had one brother, Fred, who was very spoiled. Her mother died young and her father married again.

My father farmed in partnership with his brother at Moor Farm where he also ran a riding school because he was very interested in horses. I have a photograph of him with one of his horses. He was wearing very smart livery and standing by one of the outhouses. The partnership eventually broke up and the family moved to Alford. I was four years old when we moved and, unlike my brother, Phil, who was eight at the time, I have no real memories of life on the farm or my father's parents.

The move to Alford was a crucial time in our lives. My mother was a good cook and she was going to do the catering in a restaurant/shop which was on the corner in the Market Place. The restaurant was in a large room above the shop and it was often full, especially on busy market days. There were enough bedrooms upstairs for us to have a room each. Behind the shop there was a very big sitting room, dining room and kitchen, so we were very comfortable.

Mother was very beautiful. She dressed very well and in her spare time often went to social occasions. She was very fond of dancing in spite of my father's disapproval. She used to buy some of her clothes at Coney's, the tailor's shop. I can remember a particularly beautiful skirt and jacket with a matching hat and veil which came down just over her eyes. Mum was always very good at dressmaking. She was a very special person and I think her family also regarded her as a special person. She went to a private school in Louth: Miss Field Flowers' school. That is probably why I was sent to a private school later. I do not know how she got in or out but there was always the horse and trap for transport. She lived at Panton Farm and later on at Dovecote Farm, which was not far from Moor Farm. She remembered a great deal about Louth from her school days. They were very happy days for her and she talked about them a lot.

I must have gone to school near the church because I remember stamping my foot and saying, 'Dash!' when I had difficulty in crossing the street because of the traffic. I also remember having a doll, playing 'hotch potch' in the street by the market and once I marched up the road shouting, "Does anyone here know Kelly, Kelly from the Isle of Man?" I can remember being in a gang but I don't remember their names. I do remember that we used to buy sweets from a little shop that is still there. The man who owned the shop had a stiff neck and he had to turn the whole of his body to look at the sweet jars. Another memory was visiting a man in a cottage round the corner. I talked to him a lot and sat in a ladderbacked armchair which was passed on to us and became part of our furniture.

Dad had a contract to deliver laundry. He had a horse and dray full of wicker baskets. I have vivid memories of going with him to outlying farms and crossing fords, like the one at Belchford. The horse was fed at the farms. I recall the smell of horses, the huge bins of feed and the sweet beans. These tasted of liquorice and were given to the horse. We ate some of the beans as well.

Just after the outbreak of the First World War, I went with my father to see a bomb crater near Alford. It must have made quite an impact on me because I remember wearing a pinkie red jacket and bonnet and my hand was in his. My face must have been dirty because he wiped my face with his handkerchief and it smelled of tobacco.

My father received his calling up papers for the war and this was a terrible time for the family. If he had stayed in farming, he would have been in a protected occupation. The sense of impending disaster and lack of security was on all of us as we sat together in the room above the restaurant. The new and successful project in Alford was coming to an end just as the new baby, Fred, was born. I do not remember anything of the birth but he must have been born at home.

When my father went off to war we moved to Lincoln, where Auntie Becky and Uncle Harry lived in Norris Street. Auntie Becky was Mum's youngest sister; she was always very lively and they were good friends. They supported each other because Uncle Harry had also been called up. We moved into 37 Hope Street. It was quite a nice house with a large kitchen and a front room. The bedrooms were over an extension at the back. I can remember the plum tree in the garden which never had any plums. At the bottom of the garden there was an old pigsty where we used to play. It had an old stove and we used to cook on it. I remember taking some custard powder from the cupboard and carrying it in a matchbox down the garden. It was very watery custard!

It was a great adventure living in those hard days but my mother had difficulty making ends meet. We took in a lodger and I remember us scurrying round to get a room ready. Later, Mother bought a piano because she thought we ought to be taking lessons. It was an 'upright' and stood in the front room and had crimson silk behind the fretwork panels – it was her pride and joy.

I had a very beautiful doll with a wax face. She had some

lovely dresses because Mum was very good with her needle. I was able to dress and undress her. I still had the doll in Lincoln and I loved it dearly. One day there was something of a disaster. I had been dressing the doll by an open fire and had been called away. The wax face became disfigured. When Dad came home on leave, he tried to make it 'well' again. I do not think it was badly disfigured but it was certainly flattened. I had it for ages and ages. Everyone looked forward to the time when Dad was at home because these were 'red-letter days'. He used to sit me on his knee and sing to me: 'From Wiberton to Woberton was fourteen miles' and 'To be a farmer's boy.' At one point, after Dad returned to the war, Fred fell downstairs and all the family were affected. Thankfully there was no harm done. We were very happy together in Lincoln even though we had little money. We made our own fun!

After Dad had been on leave, Geoff was born at home but I do not remember anything about it because I was sent to stay with Mum's cousins, Uncle Jack and Auntie Annie. They had a newsagent's shop on the corner of Canwick Road. (I was walking down Canwick Road recently and remembered a Christmas party in a building directly opposite to the newsagent's shop. We were in a large room sitting at long tables with food in front of us.) Their daughter, Dolly, was married to an officer, who looked very grand in his uniform. I slept with her but when Uncle Billy returned on leave, I was banished out of her bed.

Uncle Jack used to put chocolate from the shop under everyone's bed on Saturday night so that we all had a treat on Sunday morning. Auntie Annie worked in the shop. I always thought she had such beautiful hair but never guessed that it was coloured. They had a worker, who came from Belgium – there were a lot of refugees at that time – she helped in the house with the cooking and cleaning. I remember being taken to see Geoff and having my photograph taken with this lovely baby boy. At that time Fred had beautiful flaxen curls, though you would not have thought so in later years!

Uncle Alf and Mum's sister, Auntie Lottie, also lived in Lincoln. Alf did not go to war because he was a gunsmith and had a shop in Clasketgate. We often went to see them because they did not have any children of their own and so they spoiled us. We went there for Christmas and hung up our stockings with great fun and games. It was a rather peculiar house with a tiny sitting room behind the shop. The main rooms were upstairs. I recall a great big rocking chair into which two or three of us would climb – great fun!

There were Zeppelin raids over Lincoln. One night after the alarm, we were taken to South Common because the buildings were not thought to be safe. The Zeppelins were probably searching for the munition factories. I cannot remember how old I was then. Sometimes, if we were at Auntie Becky's house in a raid, we would all get under her big table.

Another of Mum's sisters, Auntie Tilly, lived in Clarina Street off Monks Road, with Uncle Tom. He also stayed at home because he worked in munitions. Will Harrison, their son, was ordained as a minister after the war. When we visited Auntie Tilly, we also went to the Arboretum, which we loved very much. One day I went into the maze and could not find my way out. Rolling down a grassy hill was a favourite game and I used to get very dirty. Once I was dressed in a beautiful white lace dress and managed to make it very muddy down the front. Mum was so cross with me that she would not let me walk with her. She made me walk in front of her all the way home because I looked such a mess!

Phil went to school at St. Andrew's School in Lincoln but I went to a private school run by Miss Graves in her home. I remember having lunch there and that Miss Graves had a very big nose. Her sister helped her in the school and they ran it together. She taught French as the 'high light' of education. As well as reading, writing and arithmetic, we were also taught deportment, manners and elocution. I went to that school until the end of the war so it was my early education.

I must have had a fetish about clothes because I can even remember what I wore: I had a black and white check coat with a fur collar and a black and white 'tammy' over one ear. I loved wearing them because my mother had made them for me. I also had black woollen stockings and black shoes, which I hated.

Uncle Will, Dad's brother, and Auntie Frances, who was very house-proud, lived in Kent Street and he also worked in munitions. Claytons in Lincoln made war planes. A family friend once told me that our family had been 'done out of a lot of money'. This was because Uncle Will had invented the stays that held up the wings on the first planes and he was never given the credit by the firm. Everybody was intent on doing their best for the country in those days. We did not think of ourselves. We only thought of what we could do for the war effort. It was a time of great hardship but we did not count it as hardship. We only counted the victories but, nevertheless, we were very much aware of the disasters.

Sometimes I did feel a bit resentful because there were Fred and Geoff to mind and it always seemed to fall to my lot rather than Phil. I objected to the privileges of the men. The demarcation lines were much stronger in those days. Girls were expected to mind the babies and to help in the house. I do not think I had a strong mother complex, just a sense of obligation to support Mum.

At the end of the war, I could hear the church bells ringing and we were looking forward to Dad coming home, but he worked in the transport section, mostly with horses, and he was still in Germany. He was away a long time after the other men came home. Other children were reunited with their Dads and were into the routine of life again but we were patiently waiting.

Uncle Harry came back from the war and his face was scarred. We were told it was frostbite. Many of the soldiers had a mosaic pattern on their skin. We seemed to think he had a halo around him because he had suffered.

Dad was released and eventually came home. There were

difficulties for us because the farm had gone and we were facing an entirely new beginning. There were hundreds of men like Dad, all looking for a new way of life.

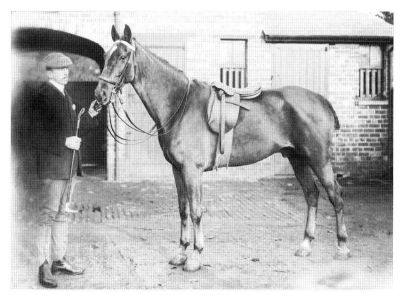

Marjorie's father Frederick with one of the horses from his riding school.

– 2 –
A New Beginning
1920s

EX-SERVICEMEN with farming experience were allocated smallholdings of ten acres in the fens of southern Lincolnshire and it was hoped that they could make a good living for themselves. It was very rich, fertile land and new houses were promised for the men and their families. The project made a very slow start. Land was available on the Carter estate but the houses were not yet built. Some holdings were bigger than others. They were twenty acres or even, in some cases, thirty acres. We moved into a wooden hut and we had ten acres. This was not really adequate for a family. Later we acquired another ten acres but even then there was not enough yield to feed and care for a family. Fred and Geoff were still at primary school. They had to walk for miles along the roads following the drains to reach the school at Eastville, in the East Fen. I went to school with them, to take care of them, both there and back.

This was not a very happy time. Our Lincoln accents were different from the fen accent and so we were 'strangers'. We did not have our family around us. There were uncomfortable adjustments all round. Dad had his horse and cart so he won a contract to cart stone for the building work. This brought in very necessary extra money but ate into the time available for the farm. All the family helped with the farm work. Sugar beet was a popular crop then because it was subsidised. Seed was allocated to the farmer and followed by a subsidy at singling, which was the thinning out of the plants. We all helped with the singling, by hand. When the crop was lifted, we helped again with the cleaning and chopping. A sample was tested at the factory for sugar content and we watched anxiously because this determined the price of the beet. Those were hard days but the family worked together.

It was wonderful when we were allocated our permanent house but there were always financial difficulties. We took in a lodger, Miss Moore, a teacher from the school and this also helped. Phil, the eldest boy, went to King Edward VI Grammar School at Spilsby. He went on the train each day so he received the most benefit from this time. I was to go to the Magdalen School at Wainfleet but I do not remember a great deal from that school, because there was a big upheaval in our lives. Dad and Mum took over another farm at Norton Disney. The land ran alongside the woods. Mum wanted a dairy herd but Dad thought it would be too tying with the milking, morning and night.

Phil and I went to live on that farm in 1925 and I suppose I was 'in charge'. I loved the old farmhouse. Eventually, Phil went driving for a local bus company and one of the routes went through Bassingham, where he met his future wife, Eve Taylor. I started going to Norton Disney chapel and I was asked to train to be a Local Preacher. All the family moved to Norton Disney and Fred and Geoff went to Mount School in Newark. They went off each morning by bus. We began to entertain Local Preachers on Sundays and I started to study for my Local Preacher's examinations.

All of us still worked on the farm. One of the crops was oats and March 12th was the date for sowing oats. There was always trouble with rabbits from the woods eating the new shoots of the crops. We went out to set the snares and early every morning there was the inspection to see what had been caught. The rabbits were sent to market and were part of our income. We grew potatoes and these were sent to Newark market for auction. We had eggs and we must have had some cows because we had milk. We separated the milk and made butter. I remember churning and hot days when the butter 'went to sleep' and would not 'come'. And days when I had difficulty keeping it cool enough. I made one pound and half pound pats. These were put in butter paper, cut to size, and rolled with a stamp.

We had a grocery man who had a horse and van. He took our eggs and butter in a barter system to pay for the groceries. The eggs had to be washed and the churning done, with everything ready for his Thursday visit. We kept White Wynedots. These were pure white hens. We incubated eggs, looked after the chickens, grew them up, and then we sold the cockerels and kept the pullets. They were a big source of income.

The carrier came to the end of the road by the woods. He picked up everything we had to sell in Newark market on Wednesdays. Then we had to go to Newark also, to Hopewell the auctioneer, waiting to see how much we had earned that week. Our spending depended upon this. If we had done well, there would be money for some extras. I took a job in Newark at Brooke's Garage and I used to cycle in. I bought myself a new bicycle at Currys and paid for it in instalments. My Dad hated this but it was the only way. I could not afford it otherwise on my wages.

By that time my Local Preacher's examinations were well under way. The lads in the study group included my cousin, Will Harrison, and the leader was Mr Jeive from St Catherine's Church, the leading church of our Circuit. We all became accredited Local Preachers and five of the lads became interested in offering for the ministry. Mr Jeive began to challenge me too by talking about the Wesley Deaconess Order. Revd Percy Bourne, the Superintendent, came to see if I really could take this up seriously.

Percy Bourne talked about the training and the candidating. He spoke about the examinations I would have to sit. He thought I should do some more advanced study in order to be ready for candidating, so that is what I began to do. It made me part of the fellowship of the lads who were already Local Preachers. They came to preach at Norton Disney and we exchanged notes. Lads like Jack Harrod, Edwin Sturdy and the Staceys, and I was the only girl in this group. I went out on Note, then on Trial and then became fully accredited. No one had his or her own transport in those days so we all used to go out on the preachers' bus. We were picked up at various points and taken to our appointments. We exchanged texts and talked about what we were going to do that day, though none of us was keen to give away our sermon outline just in case someone else used it! We were planned to go round the same churches. We did, however, tell each other our illustrations and also tall stories. I think that Local Preachers had a much greater status in those days. The Local Preacher was the minister for the day in the village. Each one went to a family who invited him to lunch after the morning service. In the afternoon we were expected to join in the Sunday School. If someone was sick we visited and sometimes we were asked to pray. After tea we took the evening service and then the bus picked us up at the pre-arranged point.

Local Preachers' Meetings were very important especially when reports were given. My recognition service was also an important occasion, in St. Catherine's Church. I began to study through a correspondence course: Old Testament, New Testament, theology and church doctrine, from 1933 to 1935. I think my tutor was a minister called Baker, because he seemed to be the minister who came to us most often. The written work is what I remember most, because the scripts were returned corrected and marked. These were the marks which were presented when I candidated.

I used to cycle the seven miles to Newark. Sometimes the roads were icy and I had several close shaves. Once I came off directly in front of a traction engine but I got up and got going again. I worked in the office and, thinking back, I must have been very inexperienced. I was the invoice clerk working with the foreman and the men. They brought their work to me and I grew to know every section of the cars very well. I had to price up the work and parts with Mr Evans, who was my boss. Sometimes I had to take my turn in the shop – at lunch times for instance. It was a great experience. The men were very good to me but I must have seemed very raw.

Attached to the garage there was a hotel, owned by Mr Ashton, a very dapper little man. He always wore a bowler hat and a bow tie but he did not do very much work. He had a housekeeper because commercial travellers working in the district used to stay. The housekeeper was a very large lady called Miss Kipp. I do not know whether she was a war refugee or not but she was Belgian and her English accent was never very good. When the winter came with the icy roads, Mrs Ashton asked if I would consider coming to stay instead of cycling in all weathers. There was a little bedroom and Miss Kipp could look after my food. The cost would come out of my wages. Mrs Ashton said it would be better for them and better for me. I said I would have to see what was happening at home but that was what I did.

They were very happy days for me. I was able to attend at Barnby Gate Methodist Church in Newark. I started to attend the Guild as I was there in the evening and I got to know the minister, Revd Bamford. I also got to know the people but I do not remember preaching in the Newark Circuit. I joined Miss Knight's class. The Knights were rich folk, who had businesses in Newark. I got to know younger people through this class and the basis of my theological training was being laid. Revd Bamford was a very good preacher and he gave very good children's addresses. My boyfriend knew how interested I was in them so he wrote them out in Old English script and illustrated them. He was one of my first boyfriends.

This was the time of my formative training. I began to save up a little because I knew there would be no money from home. The men used to tease me about my Local Preacher's work – 'my stance' as they called it. At lunchtime I went out into the town. Geoff and Fred used to go to the cattle market and we ate our sandwiches together. Then we used to buy something at Noble's pie shop at the end of Kirkgate. Mr Noble attended Barnby Gate Church and made us very welcome. He sold big round biscuits called teacakes. The tops looked as if they had been pricked with a fork. They were very filling and very tasty. That was the time we moved from Norton Disney and stopped farming at Eastville. We seemed to be paying off obligations for quite a long time. We moved to Thorpe on the Hill in 1934, where we rented a farm from the Roper family.

Prelude to Dawn

Not a breath of wind stirs...
The air is fresh and clean.
Dew covers the grass
With silvery sheen.

The sun slants over the hill.
Shadows, like long fingers pointing...
All is still.
Waiting - for the explosion of life
Dawn brings.
The cessation of movement
Before noise and strife.

Birds twitter.
The martins fly low
Feeding on the wing.
The thrush hunts silently.
None sing.
Not yet the outburst of praise
To greet the morn.

Even the sky is empty of cloud
Like a thin veiling shroud
To lift only when the day is born.

Happy Days at Thorpe on the Hill
1934 - 1941

I T WAS a very happy time for all of us, especially for Mum. We had a lovely old farmhouse in the centre of Thorpe on the Hill called St. Margaret's Farm. It had good farm buildings but the land was scattered. Across the road from the farmhouse there were grassy fields which ran right down to The Bridges. This crossed Thorpe Lane. The land went on down to Station Road. Most of the land was on the Fosse Lane and it was called The Twin Gates. We had to travel with all the implements to this land and also cross the A46 to The Dankers, which was heavy clay land. It proved to be a very difficult farm to manage. However, Mum had her way and the herd was increased and to her joy she began her dairying. She loved it.

The John Hunt Memorial Chapel was at Thorpe on the Hill. John Hunt had been a missionary to Fiji and his gown and walking stick, along with other items, were in a showcase in the entrance. There was a schoolroom at the back with a Sunday School and we also had a very lively Guild. The Guild really was the centre of the social life in the village. Dad became interested in the chapel and this was a source of great joy to Mum and she too joined the Guild. They became VIPs at the chapel and mixed very well into the social life of the village. Since I was a Local Preacher, I was also preaching at

Thorpe and the other preachers were entertained at the farm. The boys continued to go to school in Newark and I also continued to work in Newark. We walked to the station in the morning and came back together in the evening on the train.

There was a very exciting occasion when we had a 'mission' at Thorpe on the Hill. We had a missioner called Tom Jones. He was a singer. He had composed a lot of his own songs and he was Welsh. He played a little harmonium and sang his songs. He taught all his songs to the children. He had a ten-day mission and he stayed with us. People were converted during this mission. I still have his book of songs, and remember singing some of them.

Eventually I became the secretary of the Guild. At that time there was a Chairman of the District so it must have been the time when Methodism began to separate ministers to become Chairmen of Districts. It was from Thorpe on the Hill that I candidated. I could write a whole book about Thorpe, there were so many characters. There were the Ropers, for instance – Mr Roper was the village tailor and he had a shop which was absolutely fascinating. He used to do a lot of his work by hand in the shop and he sat cross-legged on the counter to do the stitching. He was a character. He grew tobacco and dried all the leaves himself and cured them. He kept bees and had honey which he sold. I do not think he was ever married. He was a little man, very knowledgeable and a wonderful tailor. I think his brother's widow was his housekeeper. She was a precise lady and in their house they had a routine which was studiously kept. Those were the days when we had to take our wireless batteries to be charged and their shop was the centre for batteries. Everyone in the village knew him.

When I was accepted for the Deaconess Order, our uniform for the students was grey and they supplied the material. Mr Roper made my first uniform. When I was ordained, I had to have another uniform and that was navy which he also made. I am still wearing those suits. We had varying patterns but we had to have hats and badges supplied by the College.

When Mr Roper was making the coat, he said to me, "Isn't this dull – all this navy! I'm going to give you a lining to cheer you up a bit." My navy coat had a gorgeous red satin lining. Once, when I was out preaching, one of the men was holding this coat for me and he said, "All glorious within". Every time I wore that coat I thought, 'All glorious within.' They were so beautifully fashioned, immaculately stitched. He is one of the characters I remember particularly.

We really were a 'dreadful' family. We made fun of people and the boys were good mimics. There was a little lady who had a sweet shop. She was very dark and the little sweet shop was very dark as well. There was a man who often used that shop to buy sweets. He was the wheelwright and was very fat. If he came to see someone, he stayed for ages and ages. We used to say, when we saw him coming, that we knew we were in for a good session. There was one incident that became a family joke. We had a long house with a great big room. There was a piano and things like that, with easy chairs as well. There was a big kitchen table in the second room, with a long dresser and a couch which ran right down one wall. By the range there was a chair with a very straight back and straight sides so that it was very narrow. Once our friend came to see us and he sat in this chair. He was a fat man and when he talked his face grew red and flustered. He got up to go but could not get out of the chair and it rose with him. We were all helpless with laughter but we could not let him see. We remembered this event every time we sat in that chair. When we got up we pretended that we were stuck – but I think, sometimes, that we overdid it!

There was a grand old house called 'Ebenezer' and it is still there. Two sisters lived there, one was a teacher at Lowdham and she came on the train with us. This was the time when women began to diet and she began to slim. She believed in fresh air and leaving the sash windows open and they did away with having tablecloths because they gathered dust. I expect we have forgotten all about that now. She got thinner and thinner and her face got thinner and thinner, so we gave her the nickname 'Ghandi'. I do not think she ever knew. People like that are never forgotten.

One of my mother's aunts, Auntie Fanny, came from London to live in Aubourn. She kept a shop and we used to go across and see her because Mum was very fond of her. She was always immaculately dressed in black alpaca but she always had a white lace collar, a gold chain round her neck and wonderful red hair. She was very 'correct' and everything was just perfect. If we went to tea there were china cups and place mats, everything beautifully set. She was a Londoner and she never lost her accent. We used to ask why she was always the same and why nothing ever changed. Mum would reply that she thought it was because she took potassium!

I never knew what potassium was, but it was supposed to keep her hair that wonderful red colour! When she died we inherited some of the things including a beautiful sideboard and a little table. I have her locket and chain and I think we also have some pieces of jet because those were the treasured things. Somehow she played a big part in our lives at that time, probably because she was different. She set this lovely standard both with eating and life itself. She became a very big part of the Methodist life in Aubourn. She was one of the Wood family.

My boyfriend began to make an appearance during the Tom Jones mission. I learned afterwards that Tom Jones had had a tremendous influence on him. While he was in Newark, he used to borrow his father's car. It was a Riley Nine and he used it to take me home sometimes. We all went to Cliff College on Whit Monday. Then, as all the lads were in training, we went to the summer school too. Cliff College is in a very beautiful setting and the prayer meetings are by the river. I remember singing this chorus:

'Stayed upon Jehovah
Hearts are fully blessed,
Finding, as He promised,
Perfect peace and rest.'
Songs of Fellowship No. 344

In that river setting it became so real and often it has come back to me, perhaps when I needed it. There were lectures and testimonies as well. It was in the time of Sam Chadwick. He had a white moustache and was not a very big man. I remember him speaking to us so it must have been when he was the Principal. I remember Norman Dunning, the next Principal, as a terrific preacher. He came to Barnby Gate Church to a Circuit rally and the chapel was full. In those days hundreds came to the Circuit rally from all around. He was a very dramatic preacher and on that occasion he took the story of Elijah on Mount Carmel testing the priests of Baal. One moment he was in one corner of the pulpit shouting, "Where's your god? He's asleep! Perhaps he's gone on a journey!" Then he was in the other corner calling down the rain. We could almost see the water running down the trenches!

We made great friendships on those summer schools. We were very intense. I had a great experience. I always think it was what Cliff College used to call 'the second blessing' and the coming of the Spirit. The experience happened in a prayer meeting in the college chapel. We were singing,

'O Thou who camest from above'.
Hymns and Psalms   No. 745

It was a visitation of the Spirit and it was associated with light all around me and in me. I remember going into the dining room with its big soaring windows and looking out on the garden and thinking that this was real. That was the seal of my calling. I knew I was called into the work. I must have had a lot of boyfriends at that time because one of them, who was in training for the ministry, proposed to me, but I was full of my own calling and he had to go.

– 4 –
Training at Ilkley
1936 - 1938

I CONTINUED with my candidating. All the preliminaries were completed but Percy Bourne said that I ought to have more practical experience. He thought that the committee would say that I lacked experience with people, so I began visiting. One person was the lady we called 'Ghandi.' Her mother had been taken ill with cancer and I went to see her in their big, old house. In this way I began to gain in experience.

Now I come to think about it, I had already had a good deal of family experience. There had been both tragedies and problems at home. Dad had blood poisoning at Norton Disney, followed by pneumonia. He was so ill we thought he was going to die. Once Fred ran into a sugar beet lorry on the road and he came off his bicycle. We found him lying unconscious by the side of the road. We had to stop a lorry and ask the driver to take him home. Our farm was behind Norton Disney Hall and to get to it we had to use the long drive which went off the A46, and then through the woods to our house. We asked the lorry driver if he would stop at the Hall. Dad was at a meeting there for tenants; he came out and said that we must not let Fred sleep. I walked him up and down until the doctor came from Collingham. He said he thought no great damage had been done but we had to keep him in bed for a time. He said he would come and see Fred again. We were worried about the possibility of brain damage but there was none. In fact, we had difficulty in keeping him in bed! Those were very tense times when I learned a great deal.

Candidating for the Wesley Deaconess Order was quite a process. When all our forms were in and references taken up, we were invited to live from Friday till Monday in the Deaconess Training College at Ilkley. It was a stone building situated in a large garden. The bedrooms were very plain with a single bed, a chest of drawers and a wardrobe. The rooms opened onto one corridor, the 'loos' and bathrooms were at one end. All the candidates were together and one could hear what was said in each cubicle room so everyone got to know each other well! They were all in a state of trauma and extremely nervous. Members of the committee took us all for long walks round the garden. They were supposed to get to know us and talk with us. It seemed to take 'years' – like everything else did. Then we were taken for even longer walks, on the moors and round the tarn, by those very gentle people who were, nevertheless, judging us.

They had to make a personal report to the Candidates' Committee on what they had gathered from our 'heart-to-heart' talks. This was based on what we had told them about our circumstances, families, reactions to relationships and a great deal more. We were all very careful about what we wore because we felt we were 'on view'. Then, in alphabetical order, we had to go before the committee. All the marks we had gathered and our reports were there. (In later years I served on a candidates' committee and I thought how 'cruel' we were.) They were all sitting in a semicircle, looking us up and down, listening to our voices, observing the way we stood, the way we spoke and how we answered questions. The Candidates' Committee was judging us every minute, every minute! It was an ordeal. On Sunday, we went, in a body, to Wells Road Church for a service. Then we had to go for prayers in the College chapel. We still felt we were under observation. We heard the result by post. We were never told whether we had been accepted at the actual weekend.

The Candidates' Committee meeting was in July and, if we were accepted, we were admitted into college in the September, when the term began. It was presumably for a two year or three year training, according to one's capacity. During my time as a student, Dr Maltby was the much-loved and respected Principal of the College and Warden of the Order. Somehow or other I think Dr Maltby was for me, though I do not think everybody was. I was always very grateful to him because I think I was judged to be too inexperienced. Perhaps he saw something more in me than other people did. I felt I had to justify his faith in me and I expect that stayed with me. It was his example that I felt was the right example. He set the standard and I always felt that I had to keep to it. I still do. We believed that the 'Maltby theology' was the real core by which to live. Dr Maltby and his brother wrote many highly influential books and pamphlets about theology at that time.

I passed the 'test' and began my training. I was already a Local Preacher but a lot of people who came were not. Acceptance had meant a complete change in my life. It meant going away from home. It meant going away from family. It meant leaving behind colleagues and friends. It meant saying to my boyfriend that this was the end. He tried to make a bargain with me by asking me to give ten years of my life to the Deaconess Order and make that final. But I explained that I could not do that if I was accepted at the end of my training because this was to be my calling in life.

You see, candidates were never fully accepted during training at that time. We were always under observation and a lot of girls went home. They were unable to face up to the rigours of probation. We were all free to go and the committee members were able to tell us if they did not think this was the work we were called to do. We always felt that we had to work hard to meet the high standards that were required and we had to promise 'life' service. If we married, we had to come out. Those were big promises to make.

I have always felt that we were one of the best-trained groups of the Order because we had such very good tutors. There was Dr Maltby who took theology and he was an expert. Then we had Mary Hunter, who was a Scot, who took the Old Testament very thoroughly; the slightest wrong emphasis and we were corrected. Mary McCord was our Home Sister and she supervised our half-day practical work. I was sent to Eldon in Leeds where some people lived in basements and kept rabbits. They hopped around the family table while the families were having their meals. One of my tasks was to run a junior club of little 'scallywags' who came from such homes. I also visited pastorally and this was all in half a day. We went by bus from Ilkley and we wore white collars and cuffs, but after we had been in Leeds for an hour they became black.

We were learning a very vital lesson. Mary McCord impressed upon us that when we knocked on a door we were never alone because God was with us. The minister for my section had a wife who suffered from rheumatic fever. When I went to visit, I was not allowed to see her and this made me very angry. I asked why I was not allowed to see her. I could understand that she might be in a lot of pain because of the illness. He said that they had received a series of students and the last one stood at the end of the bed and told his wife that 'such things were sent to try us'. His wife burst out that if God had sent such pain to her, he was a devil. I never forgot that!

These were the lessons that Mary McCord gave us. She took us for practical sessions and helped us to return to difficult situations and face the issues ourselves. We visited Middleton Asylum and I remember going back and saying that that was my very worst experience. It was the first time I had visited an asylum with its locked doors and all the murmuring. There were some women moving around in a ward making strange sounds. The worst thing was a little lady who was having hallucinations and thought she was the Queen. How do you deal with that? How do you find the 'person'? What is the use of trying to find the 'person'? They are not there – they are 'different' people. I remember Mary saying that I was only judging what I could see. A shutter had come down between that person and myself. We do not know what is going on behind that shutter. We do not know that God is not reaching there. This made a great impression on me and it has always been a tremendous help because we do not know. It is a different dimension. It is a different person. I say that to people. It has helped them to believe there is another communication. God is able to reach them.

That was the sort of training we had and its outcome of dealing with questions in a practical way. A good deal of the training relied on question and answer. For instance, Dr Maltby once asked me, 'Would you invite John the Baptist to your wedding?' It was his way of teaching. One day when I was chairman of the College, I organised a walk to Bolton Abbey. When we arrived back we realised we were late for a lecture at 5.15 p.m. I took responsibility and bore the brunt: 'It was my fault. I took them too far.' Quick as a flash, Dr Maltby responded, 'Then you repented and turned back' – using the experience as a telling illustration of his previous lecture on repentance and forgiveness! He had an infectious sense of humour and brought the best out of people. Like St. Luke, he very much valued the service of women.

We had a roll call every morning at seven o'clock and we had to be down and ready in the common room. A verse of a hymn was played and then the roll was called. We also had domestic duties to keep the College running. We did such things as getting the meals ready, mopping the hall floor and cleaning the dining room, as well as cleaning our own rooms. I had to mend the sheets in the laundry on an old sewing machine worked by a treadle. We were on a rota and took turns taking early morning prayers. There was also a quiet time, in our own rooms. We all had a label for our door which read, 'I must not be disturbed.' Such discipline stayed with us through the years and was part of our training. For most of us, being ready by seven o'clock was also a discipline!

Those of us who were Local Preachers had to go all over the Dales by bus, even when it was icy. It was like being in the army. We had to go to Skipton and change buses to go to the villages. I remember journeys to Grassington and Connington in the ice and snow. Once when I went to Connington my hostess was an old lady and in her cottage was a table and a ladderbacked chair drawn up by the fire. There was only a bit of tablecloth at one end of the table and on it there was plum bread with cheese. In Addington there was a basement with a chapel above. I remember having to cross a swing bridge over a very turbulent river, I think it was at Addington, and it began to swing. I was frightened to death. I had to come back over it again to get to the bus that night. We were not very experienced at those sorts of things and we had to change buses in Skipton. It was really dark and we had to wait there for a long time. We were tired out. When we got back to the College, the kitchen staff had left a hot supper for us but it always seemed to be macaroni cheese! (Not really my favourite...)

It was a time of great fellowship. We used to go for long walks on the moors on Saturday afternoons, coming back in the dark and seeing all the lights twinkling. The Ilkley Moors were a great place to be. If we were not preaching, we went to Wells Road Church, in full uniform. All our suits were kept well pressed. We had to watch our appearance because of the reputation of the Deaconess Order. We all had outside work to do, which was very good. I used to do a class called the CAWG, an association for working girls called the 'Christian Alliance of Women and Girls'. Dr Maltby's secretary, Margaret Statham, ran it and I was allocated to help her. The girls were all maids in the big houses and I used to visit them. It was a great experience to see their life of 'upstairs, downstairs'. Some of them had been in service to their employers for a long time and were older. It was their way of life. It taught me a lot. This gave me freedom to visit in Ilkley itself and I kept in touch with those girls. I was also kept busy with my junior 'scallywags' in Eldon as well as the visits I made in Ilkley.

I must have made an impact in Eldon. I went to preach there and remember being invited to go back again, so I think I must have been one of the students they remembered. Once I went to see a lady who was an artist in a mixed grouping. She did some wonderful paintings. I remember saying to her that I wished I could paint, particularly when I came across the moors in the autumn and saw the bracken turning; or when I went for an early morning walk and there was frost on the ground and all the streams had little icicles, it was wonderful. I remember her saying to me, "My dear, if you feel as keenly as that about it, you can paint".

There was another thing I learned. At that time, I was in charge of flower arranging. I always had a lot of work to do. I always seemed to be on the washing-up rota and things like that. However, we had difficulty with flowers in the corners of the dining room because there were such big spaces to fill. This made us gather beech leaves and preserve them. We used to wax them by covering them with wax and using a hot iron. Then we put them under the carpets to flatten them. They really did look lovely. The ideal containers were the seven-pound jars that the marmalade and jam came in. One of our 'caravan sisters' called Nora Trineman came to stay. The 'caravan sisters' used to come and stay for a night or two in between missions and they would tell us about the work they did. They were invited to a church or circuit to lead special services, visit people, organise inspiring meetings, have special events for the children and generally involve everyone in enthusiastic evangelism.

Nora said to me, "You do the flowers, don't you. These look wonderful but it's really because of the jars. Do you think I could have one?"

"Oh I'm sure you could. We've got dozens", I replied.

So she went off with one of them under her arm. Sister Mary McCord saw her.

(She was a great friend of Nora Trineman so I think Nora

told her. I only knew she was a great friend years afterwards when Mary came to the Albert Hall, Manchester as senior deaconess.)

She called me in and said in her lilting Irish accent, "I understand that you've been giving away property that does not belong to you". I couldn't. I wouldn't. I must have looked like a cheese! "Those stone jars you've been giving away, they're not yours", she said. "They're returnable and they have to be charged".

So I was hauled over the coals. She said, "It's easy to give away things that do not belong to you. It's harder to give away things that do belong to you. It's even harder to give away part of yourself". That was the only 'ticking off' I can remember.

I enjoyed being at Ilkley. I enjoyed the training. I felt that I was learning, growing and being fulfilled. I liked the discipline, the obligations and all the opportunities for questioning and discussing. I became the college chairman while I was there and it was a great honour. This was somewhat similar to being the head girl in a school. I chaired meetings and led groups. I cared for the students when they were sick, taking round medicine or drinks. I was given my own special bedroom and I enjoyed that too. I was also given confidence when one of our deaconesses, who worked in the Queen's Hall Methodist Mission, Hull, had to go into hospital for a hysterectomy. I was considered to be the most mature of the students and I went to take her place until she was well enough to go back.

Deaconesses, 1938, with Dr Maltby and his wife.
Marjorie is seated far right.

5

War Years – Hull and Nottingham
1938 - 1945

QUEEN'S HALL Methodist Church was right in the middle of Hull and it was a place which, for the most part, catered for the underprivileged. There were great congregations and there was a wonderful togetherness. There were concerts in the Queen's Hall commanding some of the best artists of the time but there was also a degree of poverty. I remember hugely successful women's meetings. The women came with their black shawls over their heads and with evidence of violence. They were bruised and battered and very much in need of comfort and a place of refuge. The youngsters were full of vitality and mischief, often hungry and very smelly. I had to open the windows in order to maintain an evening's programme because the smell was so bad. The people were great, warm-hearted, staunch and loyal. We had a very good band of voluntary helpers. For instance at Christmas we prepared meals and packed up parcels to take out to the needy. The parties we had gave such joy to the youngsters. I had an old Vindec bicycle which took me to many of the places I had to visit in Hull. They were places that were hard to find on the map. I went along Holderness Road and by the docks.

It was a time of great testing. I had a senior colleague, Mary Watson, working on the staff and Alan Roughley was the minister. He was a very understanding and kind man. The Mission was well organised. There was a Brotherhood that met on Sunday afternoons: all men gathering together in fellowship as only men can. There was a good band and there were outdoor services. It was a time when I gained in experience and maturity.

I fully expected that when Emma Tuck came back, I would be going back to College to go on with my training but in November I began to understand that I would not be going back at all. In January 1939 I was sent to the Albert Hall Methodist Mission, Nottingham. There was a complete difference in ministry from that which we had known in the Hull Mission. Nottingham Mission was, by comparison, a wealthy mission and much more middle class than the Queen's Hall in Hull. When I first went the Albert Hall had alongside it the Institute. There were about six hundred people in full membership in the Nottingham Mission. All of them were gathered into the classes which met in the afternoons and evenings. They were full of young women and men in strong fellowship.

All the rooms were full to capacity in all kinds of groups, every day and every evening of the week. Our congregations often numbered two thousand in the evening and were gathered from all over the city. Osborn Gregory was the minister at that time and he was a wonderful preacher and a great personality. He could move that huge congregation of two thousand into laughter one minute and in the next into tears.

The Deaconesses had their own rooms in the Institute part of the Mission. We were really pampered at the beginning. We had fires lit in our rooms in the mornings by the caretakers. We could have lunch in our rooms if we wished. It really was luxurious. We could have lived there. We had our own bathroom and toilets in a little wing that was up the stairs from the entrance hall of the Institute. From there we were easily available for the people who came to talk to us. I expect those were the days when counselling was not called counselling but it was a great part of our work. There was also the pastoral visiting throughout Nottingham. The youth work was very lively. Young people gathered in the gymnasium for gymnastics and billiard tables were there as well. It was very well equipped. There was always a good Guild and the Women's Fellowships were very good. The classes were the heart of the fellowship because real teaching was going on in them all the time and the bonds of loyalty were strengthened.

It was in September 1939 that the Second World War broke out and very soon the whole scene changed. The Army requisitioned the Institute. It was going to be used by the American soldiers who were injured and sent home for recuperation. All that huge part of the building was taken from us. We only had the Albert Hall itself with the small rooms around it and the gymnasium. We were able to black out the gymnasium much more easily so that a lot of our activities were transferred downstairs into that area. I remember most of our work with young people taking place down there. Alongside the road going up to the Albert Hall there was a kind of annexe that we began to use. The upstairs rooms were used for class meetings and down below there was a used clothes store. People came to us to be fitted out for the winter. Sometimes people were fed, given money for food or sent to another place for help.

There was great upset in our congregation because people were being called up for service in the Armed Forces. People were losing their jobs or being sent to other jobs in other towns. There was great alarm among our younger people facing the threat of war and wondering what it would mean for them.

We were given rooms of our own but they were little 'cubby holes'. I had a tiny room that had been the caretaker's office. It was almost at the back entrance of the Albert Hall. I had a desk, a chair and two easy chairs. Hot water pipes were the only heating. A constant stream of visitors came to see us when we were there.

Our congregations declined because we could not black out

the Albert Hall. A lot of our evening services were held in the gymnasium. There were raids in Nottingham and we had to find shelter. Clarice Slater, who was the deaconess at Broad Street Church, and I had a suite of rooms each in a house in Magdala Road. It was a tall, round, tower-like building at the corner. It was no longer safe for us to be there so we moved to a flat in Baker Street. However, that had no adequate shelter either. When the siren sounded, we could only go downstairs and hide under the stairs. In the end, we went to sleep in the Oliver Hind Boys' Club, which had been an old asylum and we slept in the cells. We were still not free from danger there. There was a great blast in the club when there was an air raid over the Lace Market and it was on fire. I remember running across the Lace Market clutching a missionary box because I felt responsible. This was money that was not my own and I had to take care of it. The black-out restricted our coming and going in the evenings.

We suffered much sadness and change due to the war. My brothers, Geoff and Fred, were conscripted. They were called up from the Thorpe on the Hill Farm. At that time they were both apprentices in engineering. Geoff was at Ruston Hornsby and Fred was at Ruston Bucyrus. Although I think Dad hoped to keep one of the boys to work on the farm, they were both called up. My elder brother, Phil, had already volunteered. He was that kind of person and he was already in the army. He was commissioned and became a Lieutenant Colonel. Geoff went into the RAF and Fred was in the Royal Engineers. As all three were away, Mum and Dad moved from Thorpe on the Hill and gave up the farm. It was almost impossible to keep it going without the aid of the boys so they bought a place on Brant Road in Lincoln in 1941. It had belonged to my uncle some years before. It came on the market and they bought it. We did not know when they moved. It is hard to realise now what a complete blackout there was on news during the war. It was a great surprise to us when we knew that they had moved and were established in Brant Road. There was good land, meadowland going down to the River Witham. They settled there and gradually established a herd of dairy cows. In fact, the farm was called Asholme Dairy Farm.

I recall something from Nottingham that was etched in my memory. My brother Fred was in Greece, dispatch riding in Argos. His group was moved over to Crete but they were not able to defend Crete because the Germans invaded almost immediately. Fred was listed among those soldiers who were missing. In those days, of course, this sort of news was coming to families everywhere. Well, it came to us and for two and a half years Fred was missing. One evening, I was in my 'cubby hole' and a woman came to show me a little slip of paper. She said that she had found it in the *Nottingham Evening Post*. She wondered if it could possibly be my brother. And it was! It was Fred's rank number. He was a prisoner of war in Austria. We were able to get in touch with him through the British Red Cross and to send out food parcels and communicate with him.

It was a happy time for me in Nottingham. The people were very responsive and quick to take up new ideas. I think it was because they had a lot of French blood in their veins. People had come over from the Flemish areas to begin the lace trade in Nottingham. The girls were very smart. They knew how to make their own clothes. It is still the centre of the 'Rag Trade.' It always has been a lovely city and a good place to be. Even now the city is brilliant for music.

I was the district secretary for the Women's Fellowship, which was just building up at that time. I was only a probationer deaconess and when on probation we wore a light grey uniform. After we had completed our probation we were ordained. Our Convocation, which is what we call the yearly gathering of deaconesses, could not be held in the usual way during the war and we met in areas. I was ordained with the group which trained the year before me, in Plymouth. I was changed from 'a little grey sister' to 'a sister in blue' because that was when we began to wear the navy uniform.

In 1945 I was moved out of Nottingham. In the Deaconess

Order we did not choose where we would go, our committees decided for us. The Warden of the Order had a great deal of influence in this matter. I was sent to Liverpool, to the Linacre Mission, as it is now called. It was known as the Walker Mission then. It was in Litherland Road behind the docks, in the Seaforth area of Liverpool. The Mission had been handed over by the Walkers to the Methodist Church. A minister called Bill Basham was sent there to rebuild the Mission in the area after the war. That part of Liverpool had been very badly bombed and there were great tragedies. The Bryant and May factory had received a direct hit. Five hundred people had been sheltering beneath it and they were caught in this dreadful attack. Most of the children had been evacuated from the area and their house windows were boarded up. People began to come back to their homes with their children so the schools began to start up again, and the work of the Mission began to be rebuilt.

A. J. Walker had a tremendous vision. He had built the Mission in a huge, circular style in the main worship hall. Behind it was the senior hall where the teenagers met. Over the way, there was a huge building that housed Brownies, Guides and Scouts. They all had their own rooms and their own equipment. It was a vision for the future. But during the war all that part of the outer activities of the Mission stopped. These buildings were confiscated and the soldiers who were billeted in the area used part of the Mission as a canteen. It was called the 'Soldiers' Club'. Here people fed them and gave them cups of tea and they met together for a bit of entertainment.

My brother Phil stayed in India with the army after the war. Unfortunately, his last letter dated 1946, in which he said he was hoping to come home, was the last we heard from him.

6

Post War – Liverpool and Bristol
1945 - 1955

THE PEOPLE began to return and the Liverpool Mission was a centre of activity. It had a reputation for mission work. There was a tremendous Band of Hope, for instance, because drunkenness was very rife in the area. A full orchestra of very talented people led its services. Some years later, an organ was installed in the Linacre Mission in memory of A. J. Walker. Even then the orchestra and the organ led the services together. They were lively and instructive services. Building up the Mission was a tremendous task, and hard work, but very rewarding. We built up the women's meetings again. The services were also built up. We had all sorts of social activities. The Guild started again and I started a youth club. There was a great variety of activities with tremendous success at that time.

Families began to return to their homes. That part of Liverpool had always been known as a close community. When the Council rebuilt the houses, they just moved the people out for a time and then brought them back into the same area. This meant that the family grouping was never broken up. That is why the Linacre Mission has remained such an outgoing mission. Other central missions in big cities have had to close because people have moved away. People have never really moved away from around the Linacre

Mission. I went back to preach a little while ago and found the same warm fellowship and the same out-going work being done. The Mission is meeting the needs of the people in all the areas round about. Waterloo, the seafront, has been made into landscaped gardens. It is a very different area of Liverpool now.

The people who lived there at the end of the war had very little in the way of gardens. I remember going home for the day on the train so that Mum and I could go to the woods which were carpeted with primroses. We gathered big bunches of primroses and some roots as well, I must confess, and I took them back to Liverpool in a suitcase! At the Sisterhood anniversary we had little tables in the hall and we had what we called a 'Primrose Tea'. Every table was decorated with bunches of primroses. Some of the women had never seen primroses before. They had never smelt that wonderful, delicate fragrance that primroses have. In times like these we all came together in one great family. I loved Liverpool. I loved being near the water. I loved being able to get over to the Wirral. I loved all the interchange of races in Liverpool and the courage of those people who lived through those dark days and built the community up again.

It was very difficult for me to find anywhere to live when I first went to Liverpool because it was the time when the men were coming back from the war. I would probably be in 'digs' for about six weeks and then the man would return; there was no room for me, and I would have to move. I eventually found 'digs' in a street next to the Mission with a Mrs Musker who ran a canteen on the docks. This was in the time when finding food was very difficult because there was still rationing. She was able to get plenty of food because she fed the dockers. So in those days, I had the benefit of living near to the Mission, where no transport was needed, and also from being with a woman who cared for me in every way and fed me bountifully in the days when we might have found it difficult.

My sister-in-law Joan and her little girl came to stay with

Women in costumes of other countries at an International Market in Liverpool c. 1948. Marjorie is standing on the right.

me and I remember Heather being taken into the city where the trams were running at that time. She refused to board a tram and we could not understand why, until she said, 'No wheels. No wheels!' Not many trams are running in Liverpool now!

It has changed considerably since then, except for its warm atmosphere and its feeling of tradition through the ages. It is the same river and there are the same ships. I remember being on the Prince's landing stage when people were emigrating to Australia, as a lot of people did then. It seemed that there was no work for them to do in our country. I was waving off, with the rest of the families, the people who were going out there to try and make a new start. Families were separated.

This time at Linacre was a time of growing together and initiating things like the fund-raisers called the 'Italian Market' and the 'International Market,' when we had all the women wearing costumes representing other countries. All the stall-holders dressed in brightly coloured costumes. There were all kinds of stalls: cakes, sweets, toiletries, market produce, linen goods, hand knitteds, clothes, books, refreshments and games. The markets spoke practically about great days of initiative and rebuilding.

From Liverpool I moved into a very different kind of work and atmosphere. I was sent to Bristol. In Bristol there was one of the first ecumenical experiments. It was in East Bristol in Redfield. All the churches along the main road came together in one team. There were Anglicans, Methodists and Congregationalists from their churches, and the Baptist minister agreed to sit in the meetings when he could. They had agreed that the young people in all those churches should be gathered together in one youth centre. It was called the Redfield United Front. The Revd Mervyn Stockwood was the leader of the team. I went to Bristol in 1950 to be the youth organiser in the centre. It was a great pioneering experiment.

It was at a time when the government provided money for

work among young people between the ages of 14 and 20. The Bristol Education Committee paid my salary. The Youth Committee was a subcommittee of the Bristol Education Committee. In our youth centre we had about three hundred and fifty young people, and I had an assistant leader who was a man. We were really very fortunate in our youth centre, in that we were able to command good tutors. Our drama group, for instance, competed in the Cheltenham Festival. Our football teams had coaching from Bert Cann who was the coach for Bristol Rovers. We were able to organise holidays, one abroad and one in this country, every year. We ran the youth centre on a parliamentary system so the youngsters elected their own 'members of parliament'. They were responsible for ideas and the discipline of the club, which was much stricter than anything we would have inflicted upon them. It was a great social occasion.

We also had a community house for our older students and we did 'A level' coaching there, in a more informal atmosphere. Our ministerial team met every Tuesday morning for communion and then we had breakfast together. There were no barriers. The man who cooked breakfast and served us had been a batman during the war. All our ministers came together. Tuesday night in the youth centre was church night. On that night we came together and looked at our beliefs. We said to our young people, 'We want you to be committed to membership but you can choose whatever denomination you like and whatever worship you like: High Church, Low Church, Congregational, Baptist or Methodist, we are all one team'. It was a wonderful experience.

On Whit Monday we used to have a great open-air sports day and it was properly done. Courses for races were mapped out correctly and races were timed. When we were preparing for it, we always had an eye on the weather – What would we do? We had five hundred people to cater for. What if it was wet? What would we do? There were all those anxieties but great times of joy mixing with those youngsters. I candidated for the ministry when I was in Newcastle but I was ordained in Bristol. When I was ordained, a lot of those youngsters, who had been part of the Redfield Youth Centre, were at my ordination. It was a great 'match making' area and a lot of them had married each other by that time and had families of their own.

Two events in my life happened while I was working in Bristol. One was that I was not very well and when I went to the doctor she told me that, probably, I would have to have an operation: a hysterectomy. I was anxious to put that off for a while because the Wesley Deaconess Convocation was taking place in Bristol and I was the accommodation secretary. We were very busy but, as it happened, a little while before the Convocation, which was to take place in April, I had a haemorrhage. I was taken into hospital in Bristol. My surgeon, who was recommended by my doctor, was a woman named Mary Potter. She was away when I was taken into hospital so I had to wait a while before she could operate. When she did operate, it was a hysterectomy. I was in hospital when Convocation took place in Bristol. I received many letters and messages of condolence because I had to miss the Convocation. I went to Bournemouth for a little while to convalesce and then I went home. When I arrived home, I found that Mum was not very well. Through our local doctor I got her to a specialist and the news was not very good. She had had pernicious anaemia for some time and had been receiving injections. She had not been very well. We knew that her pancreas was not working properly. We did not want to alarm her, though the specialist's advice was not good news and we thought that perhaps it was cancer. I returned to Bristol and came home on holiday in July to find Mum much worse.

I returned to take charge of the youth centre again, from September to October, so that we could arrange for somebody to take my place. I knew that I had to go home to nurse Mum. The doctor had said that she would grow progressively worse. I went home in October and Mum died on December 23rd. I stayed at home with Dad and Fred until March 1954 and then went back to Bristol. The temporary youth leader finished his work there and I took over again until 1955.

In the July I was told that I would be going to work in Manchester. The committee of the boys' and girls' clubs had asked if I could be given permission to stay. I would work in another part of Bristol in another type of youth centre. The Wesley Deaconess Order thought that I ought to move into another kind of work. Revd Norman Dawson was my minister in the Redfield Methodist Church. When our advice came as to where we would be moved to in July, mine was to the Manchester Mission. Norman Dawson was very angry with this because he thought it would be putting me back into the kind of work I had outgrown.

As a matter of fact, it was another pioneering job. I would be working from the Peter Street branch of the Manchester Mission, the Albert Hall. Bill Gowland had been the minister there and had opened up a new kind of work in industry. He had pioneered an industrial chaplaincy in the firm of Small and Parkes. They were part of the Asbestos Group and they made brake linings for cars. Bowden Parkes was a member of our Methodist church. It was he who invited Bill Gowland to go into the factory of Small and Parkes, which was in the Harperhay area of Manchester, as chaplain. Bill had earlier opened up Industrial Chaplaincy. Later, it became an ecumenical team led by the Bishop of Middleton. He had pioneered industrial work in the Sheffield Industrial Mission. It was a strange kind of appointment for a woman. A man had been working on the team but I was the first woman to work in Small and Parkes. We were well-known there. I became a member of the ecumenical team.

7

Industrial Chaplain – Manchester
1955 - 1963

I WOULD BE working as an industrial chaplain from the Albert Hall in Peter Street. I was part of the staff which meant that I also had other work to do. I had a group of young people which met on Tuesdays for instance. Into that group, which was very outgoing, I could introduce people whom I met in the varying firms and knew that they would be warmly accepted. It was the kind of atmosphere where they could feel at home. Many of those young people were also members of what we called the 'Mobile Squad'. They went out on Saturdays to give help, wherever help was needed, amongst my contacts in industry. This even included cleaning, decorating and refurbishment for those living alone.

I became involved with the ecumenical team and my factories included Small and Parkes. They had a group of weavers because some of the asbestos brake lining belts were woven with cotton, zinc and brass. Other brake linings were made with a dust background which was baked together to make it hard. The men worked in long lines and I visited on the factory floor and also in the canteens and the offices. We had to have continuity in our factory visiting, always going into the factory on the same day in the week. We went in by permission of the management and also of the shop floor and the trade unions. This meant that we were accepted in every part of the factory. Small and Parkes was a very friendly group and they accepted me and I was always very grateful to them. We had to earn our right to speak, of course, getting to know more about the workings of the factory than the men did themselves. Very often they only worked in a part of the factory and we saw the finished product. We had to know enough about the factory to understand how the men worked and what was expected of them. We tried to bridge the gaps that often existed between the men who worked on the factory floor and the office staff, management and personnel, to bring the whole work force together as a group.

I remember one particular incident in Small and Parkes. We had to check in with the commissionaires at the gate. One day when I went in, they asked me if I would look at the racing lists. 'Put a pin in', they said, 'See if you have any luck with a winner!' The Rootes Group owned another of my factories and I had a man there who followed racing. He studied form and was quite knowledgeable so he often gave me 'tips'. On the Tuesday when I had been into the Rootes Group, he had given me a 'tip' which he said was worth backing. I said to the commissionaires, 'Perhaps I can do better than put a pin in. I can give you a good 'tip' that was passed on to me'. They were very happy about this. About a quarter past three in the afternoon, all round the factory my name was being paged. It was to give a message to the chaplain to tell her that the 'tip' I had given had come up and the horse had won! I was in danger of being more popular as a 'tipster' than as a chaplain but it all helped me to be accepted in the factory.

My factories also included Broads. Jesse Broads was an old-established firm where they did leather work, ledgers and gold scrolled writing. There was a long history of very skilled people. They also had up-to-date printing machines and did the colour brochures for the British Motor Show. I worked at Jesse Broads when the whole thing was changing. This was when they were introducing colour printing and when the old method of engraving was being changed to photography. There were divisions in the printing trade and the master printers were often quite loath to employ apprentices. There were five unions operating in that factory so tensions were often quite high.

I was also in Small and Parkes when the management was changed because disc brakes were coming into fashion. An American method of moulding was introduced into the factory. This meant the introduction of new machinery, followed by a lot of redundancies. It was a very hard time when the men were made redundant. Some of them had worked in the factory from being teenagers. There was also another hazard in Small and Parkes. It was asbestos. The men had to be under close medical supervision and they had a daily ration of milk to protect them against the insidious asbestos needles that penetrated into the lungs. This was a bit like the troubles in mining. Several of our men were ill and some of them were terminally ill.

The Methodist method of working in industry was a little different from that of the Anglican Church. The Anglican chaplain believed that his ministry was just to the man at work. We believed that it was to the whole man because what happened at home had repercussions in his work. We followed up with home visitation and, if there was trouble at home, then we went to listen to see if there was anything that could be done to help. Gradually I built up a large list of contacts made during my factory visiting.

Another of my factories was in Trafford Park – British Insulated Calendars Cables. They were responsible for high tension cables and laying underwater telephone cables. It was a factory that had been known as Glover's Cables. It was an old-established firm with many routines and rules. They had division of the canteens: the men workers, the women workers on the factory floor, the junior office workers, and the young executives. In the canteens, it was said, they went from tables with no tablecloths to damask tablecloths, Turkish carpets and silver cigarette boxes! There was quite a class distinction. All that went when British Insulated Calendars Cables took over. The divisions were not acknowledged but were still kept. Although the walls of the canteen were broken down, the people still sat with the same group to which they were accustomed. Another of my factories was the Rootes Group, the car group, and in the Manchester factory they made the British Telecom long vans. They built the vans on long chassis. The group employed very experienced men. It was while I was working at the Rootes Group that I learned how to drive and I passed my driving test in Manchester.

Another of the pioneer jobs I did when I was in Manchester was work among school leavers. We felt that school leavers ought to be prepared for the transition from school to work and that such preparation ought to begin in the fourth form. In the Newton Heath Further Education College there was a man called Raoul Harrison who was the Principal. He was prepared to help and he used the College to hold conferences which helped in this transition. We got together and co-ordinated a committee consisting of careers teachers from the schools, youth employment officers and supervisors on the factory floor. Also included were some of the fourth form teachers whose pupils would be school leavers in the summer. All of them worked in liaison in that part of Manchester. Some of the factories such as Mather and Platt, were very, very good in supporting us. In those conferences we had the young people who were about to leave and looking for work. We grew to know their interests. We asked people who had been at work for a year or so to talk to them. The supervisors who would be in charge of the school leavers when they did go to work also explained their work. The various factories provided people who talked about the kind of work which would be available to the youngsters. It was pioneer work and it met with very great success. The school leavers' conferences attracted a great deal of attention and they did the work for which they were intended. They helped the school leavers in the transition from school to work. Out of that experiment came the idea of work experience. The young people went into the factory or to a shop or into other work for a short time, say fourteen days, just to find out what it was like. Some

Parading with the Albert Hall banner in Manchester.

The 'Mobile Squad' in Manchester.

of the youngsters would say they were learning, 'To work hard all day'! We had house groups as well and sometimes, if a question arose in an area or if there had been an accident at work and the friends and relatives were asking questions, we had a house group with them where people could talk. We also had a very good ecumenical team where we met and shared our experiences and learned from each other. We also had all sorts of conferences where we talked about the big questions that were arising in industry at the time.

Working on the staff of the Albert Hall brought me into contact with the great congregation there. I realised that often our church services were not really very relevant to our people at work. Often I was the only link between the church and industry. The men said that I was a catalyst and often they were envious of the style of life that I led. It was not possible for them because life, as they often said, was just one compromise after another. What they hoped for was a win on the 'pools'or something to get them out of the rut they were in, lifting them out of the 'rat race' as they said. They always wanted their children to have a better education than they had experienced themselves and a better start in life.

Instead of a harvest festival we had an industrial festival and we brought into the Albert Hall representatives from industry. The firms were very good. They brought into the Hall an exhibition that showed the range of methods of work in their factories. Hall and Pickles brought precision tools. The weavers and the bookbinders came. Turners of Trafford Park, who also dealt in asbestos, came. People who built tractors and the car manufacturers manned displays. We had Ukrainians working in the factories and they had a very good male voice choir. We invited them to come along to the industrial festival in their national costumes and sing for us. We had the Halle Orchestra, of course, just over the way and they came to play for us. The men came to the industrial festival because this was their kind of harvest. This was the work they did. This was the manifestation of their skills. They were not used to church services but, providing that we had a printed hymn sheet that showed the order of service so that they knew what to do, then they felt comfortable.

In the Albert Hall on a Saturday night we had a variety of concerts. They usually had a national flavour. For instance, we had a Scottish concert and a Welsh concert, using national songs. Percy Scott was the Principal of the Hartley Victoria Training College and we often took the ministers who were in training there round the factories and showed them how an industrial chaplain worked. I had known Percy Scott for a long time. The Scots were farmers at South Clifton when we were farmers at Thorpe on the Hill. Reg.Walker, who was the minister at the Albert Hall at that time, wanted to set up a puzzle corner. This meant that questions could be received from the audience on Saturday nights and then answered from the platform. Percy Scott and I were asked if we would be responsible for the puzzle corner. A big placard was set up on the stage and we sat underneath it and answered the questions that came to us on 'Saturday Night at the Albert', as it was called.

There were lots of activities in this industrial work that were absolutely new and exciting. It involved also the mothers' and babies' home, several kinds of mission and the holiday home for children in Prestatyn. Whenever there were big issues raised in the city of Manchester, the mission had a part to play. This was as well as its evangelical work and its work amongst young people. It was recognised as a great force in that great city.

I enjoyed working at Manchester. There were four of us deaconesses who shared a house in the Whalley Range area of the city. We each had our own rooms which were bedroom and sitting room combined. There was a lovely garden as it was one of the old houses in Whalley Range. We shared the kitchen. That was good because we had a background. We were all in the same kind of work in different parts of the city and we shared a lot of our traumas and our joys. We had great fellowship together. The house was within an easy bus ride of the city centre so this meant that our transport, getting to and from our home, was easy. That is what it was – our home. The Whalley Range area was a very well-respected residential area at one time but it has deteriorated over time.

I was fortunate in having the team at the Albert Hall backing me in the work that I did in industry. I had my own room there and I could use it for meeting people. That was a very warm fellowship. We worked together and I was part of the staff meeting and that gave me great encouragement in the work that I did. I still keep in touch with many of the people that I grew to know in industry. A lot of the younger people have moved out from the centre of the city into areas like Sale and Timperley but they have continued to play their part and witness in the new areas where they now live.

January

The sun is rising over a snow white world.
Glistening with ice spangled light.

The birds on the roof tops
Are standing in a row – one-legged –
Facing towards the East – packed tight.

Are they warming up? In conference?
Or worshipping?

Silent, together, in formation
And still.

Concentration evident from tail to bill.

An example set for people like me
To start the day acknowledging
The source of all we see.

– 8 –
Brimington and Lincoln
1963 - 1972

I COMPLETED eight years in Manchester and in 1963 I was moved out again and sent into a pastoral charge. It was in Brimington, two and a half miles from Chesterfield and about 40 miles from Lincoln. I had a home in a maisonette not far from the crematorium, which was just over the road. In fact, while I was in Brimington I served on the crematorium rota. I had bought a car. It was a Standard Nine. There was no garage at my home so I kept it at the crematorium. It was always out in the open and I could see it from my window in the flat. It was a good little car and had plenty of much needed horsepower because in Brimington there were hills. The Staveley Iron Works were not very far away and there was a lot of very heavy traffic. Often when I got behind that traffic I had to crawl up the hills and needed quite a bit of extra horsepower.

I was sent to Brimington at a very interesting time because there was a scheme to bring together several of the churches. They had been built and had existed under the splinter groups of Methodism, but had come together in one Methodist Church in 1932. They included the old Primitive Methodist Church, 'Mt Zion', the United Methodist Church, 'Bethesda', and the Wesleyan Methodist Church, 'Trinity'. The scheme was to sell some of these churches and build a new church, which would be known as the 'Methodist Church in Brimington'. 'Bethesda' was sold and became a garage. People gathered together for worship and church fellowship in 'Trinity' church. It was decided that as the site of the old 'Mt Zion' church was in the centre of Brimington and had more space around it than the others, that would be the site of the new building.

We began to plan for that and people joined together to prepare for the united cause. I was in pastoral charge. I was the minister in all but name and therefore I was given a dispensation to administer the sacrament. I never felt very happy with this expediency. We were given this privilege because of the shortage of ministers in ministerial charge and the fact that we had churches which needed someone to administer the sacrament. I also had pastoral charge at New Brimington. There was a lively fellowship at Brimington with some very good lay leaders and there was a very good group of young people with enterprising youth leaders. I went in the September and soon learned of all the new pastoral duties that were my charge.

In November I had news that my father had had a heart attack. I used my car and travelled home straight away. We had a family doctor, Tom Chapman. He rang me to say that since my mother had died and my father and brother were alone on the farm, he knew that Dad would need nursing and that I would have to come home. I thought, when I saw him, that that was true. That would really be the end of my ministry because he would need nursing. I was the only girl in the family and he needed me. I would have to make myself available.

The people at Brimington were very unhappy when they heard this because they felt they were in a state of flux and about to build a new church. They had a lot of negotiations of buying and selling and money to be raised. They thought that I had promised to leave my father and my mother and to serve the church and therefore I ought to remain with them. It was very difficult for us to get somebody to fill my place. There was a shortage of both ministers and deaconesses, so for a time I went backwards and forwards from my home on Brant Road, Lincoln to Brimington. I took essential services at the weekends and often fellowship meetings in the middle of the week. I remember that my brother took me over on Christmas Day to take the Christmas morning service. I did that until Sister Dorothy Carey became available. She came and took over my work and my place. I went home to look after my brother, the farm and to nurse Dad.

I thought that would be the end of my ministry but it was not. Tom Earis, who was the Superintendent in the Lincoln South Circuit, was based at St Catherine's Church. He asked if I could look after Dad and also give some pastoral care to two causes in Hykeham: Moor Lane and the Village. Hykeham Village Church was a small cause in the centre of the village. Moor Lane was our church nearer to the Health Centre and the schools further up in the village. That is what I did. I had pastoral charge of those two village causes. There were classes, preaching appointments, women's meetings, mums' and toddlers' clubs, baptisms, weddings and funerals to take from those centres.

In 1965, work began on the Birchwood estate. Plans were made to build a new church there. I went to do some work at Birchwood. We had our services in the Anglican Church, which was built of wood at that time. We began to have our meetings in the school and a lot of house meetings to build up the work. There was a lot of visiting to be done because there were so many people moving into the estate. In the end our new church, a very beautiful church, was built at Birchwood and I was there at the opening ceremony. The Revd Donald Baddley was the minister at St Catherine's Church then and he was in charge of Birchwood. I worked there when the new church was opened and in the activities there.

A new venture began in Lincoln in 1967 – the Lincoln City Centre Team Ministry (LCCTM). This was to be an ecumenical venture taking in all the denominations and working together as a team. The hub was to be in the Centre with the spokes radiating out into all the activities in Lincoln. These would include education, social work and industry. It was a great vision. Geoffrey Eddy, who was our Chairman of the District at that time, asked if I would work with John Willcox. He was the industrial chaplain and the Anglican vicar of the church in Cameringham. I was to work alongside him in industry and also be a member of the team. It was a great opportunity. At first we had our office in the Congregational Church in Newland. Then it was decided to alter the church of St Mary le Wigford so that we could have an office there. We could also partition off part of the church to make a room for several organisations to have a centre there. We could also use the St Mary le Wigford church hall for our outgoing activities.

The Revd Stanley Booth Clibbon was our first leader and he and his family came to live in Lincoln. He had had experience of working ecumenically in Kenya and so he came to be our leader. We met as a team at the YMCA on a Tuesday morning for breakfast. The YMCA was part of our outreach work as well. We also had team communion, of course. We had the ministers from the Congregational Church, St Andrew's, the Presbyterian Church and John Dennis from St Swithin's. We also had social workers working with us. Brian Baker was our worker in education and John Willcox was our industrial chaplain in the factories.

I began work in Rustons, Dorman Diesels, the Beever Foundry and Clayton de Wandre. Then it was thought that we might do some chaplaincy in commercial places. We gained entry into Marks and Spencer, Woolworths and the Halifax. This was a different kind of ministry because we could not go onto the factory floor. We had to work in the canteens. Since this was a special time of freedom for workers, we had to be careful not to invade the privacy of people. Marks and Spencer had training periods from 8.30 in the morning and we could go into those sessions. It was a great opportunity to meet people at work. They were appreciative and they helped us in the team ministry.

There was a small hall in St Mary le Wigford Church. This was right in the centre of Lincoln so on Friday mornings we began to serve lunches. It was at 12.30 and we had a team of people who helped us to prepare it. Afterwards we had speakers. Whatever big questions were important in Lincoln at that time, we debated them. This became quite an important part of our work. People came into Lincoln on Friday, which was market day, and came in to see us in the Lincoln City Centre Team Ministry.

During all this time I was able to live at home. This was a great opportunity because it meant I could look after my brother. My father died in May 1975 and I was able to stay with Fred and continue my work with the team ministry. It was a great advantage. My other brother was living in Hykeham at that time. Later they moved out to Skellingthorpe. Geoff came out of industry and my sister-in-law, who had a shop in Hykeham, also retired. This meant they had more leisure to be with Fred and they took a little bit of the pressure from me.

Revd Stanley Booth Clibbon, who was our leader, left us to be in charge of St Mary's, Cambridge and we had to look for a new leader. Revd John Hammersley eventually came to be that leader but in the time between, almost a year, I was elected leader of the LCCTM It was a great responsibility but a great privilege and a wonderful opportunity to see that our team as a team was successful. This experiment in Lincoln still continues but in a rather different guise as the Lincoln Group Ministry. Since I have come back to Lincoln, I have been down to St Mary le Wigford for their Friday lunch and musical events. I find some of the same people working there and that the work, in some measure, is still going on.

While I was working in the LCCTM I was based at our Central Methodist Church on the High Street. I was part of their Circuit Meeting and I preached around the Circuits. That gave me an opportunity to tell people about the work of the LCCTM Looking over the Brayford now, at the new university building, I am reminded that one of the places I visited as industrial chaplain, was the Hovis Mill. It stood on the side of the Brayford and all of the grain came in by boat. It was tunnelled into the factory where all the flour processes began. I remember especially that all of the channels, through which the flour went, were made of pinewood. These were made in the carpenters' shop and there was the lovely smell of pine in that room because the floors were covered in pine shavings. The owners of Hovis Mill moved the entire staff to Selby not very long after we began industrial chaplaincy there. It was a warm and intimate group of people who worked there. Now, of course, the Hovis Mill is destroyed and no longer a feature of the Brayford.

My weeks were pretty full. I was at Marks and Spencer at half past nine on Monday mornings and at Woolworths at 3.45 in the afternoon. I went to Claytons on Tuesday and Rustons on Wednesday. On Thursday morning, I went to the Halifax and I was at the Hovis Mill on Friday. All the commitments, which being in team ministry involved, were fitted round these fixed times for visiting. One of the things we had to promise when we started industrial and commercial chaplaincy, was that we were consistent in our visitation. We tried very hard not to alter the day or the time that we were using to go into the factory or offices. Those days were very busy days.

It was a busy time on the farm as well because there was the milk quota and dairy farming was still in progress. Fred had casual labour to help him at that time. He had begun to diversify a little. Sugar beet, for instance, gave place to crops that could be sold at the door. He had quite a business selling vegetables, potatoes and fruit. One year he had a very big crop of strawberries which was sold from the door. When the fruit season was in and the gooseberries, plums and apples were ripe, there was quite a busy time bottling and jamming to preserve them. It was really a very challenging time of my life with so many varied interests and also a lot of commitment and responsibility.

Auntie Becky, my mother's youngest sister who lived at Waddington, was taken ill with a heart attack on August 29th 1972. Joan and Geoff were away on holiday, so Fred and I were responsible. I had to get in a nurse and doctor because she was too ill to be taken to hospital. She died on August 31st. Fred and I had to arrange the funeral. Herbert Millington, who lived with Auntie Becky, had been one of their proteges from his teenage years and he helped us. The funeral service was held at Waddington Church and she was buried in Waddington cemetery. Herbert came and stayed with Fred and me at Brant Road over that difficult time.

There was a Deaconess Convocation at that time, as well as many industrial conferences with which we had to keep in touch. I have also been looking through all the titles of our Friday lunch debates which were, to say the least, very interesting and we really did tackle the big questions of that time.

My commitment to Fred was rather lessened because Joan and Geoff were available and he was becoming more independent and looking to change the whole pattern of work at Brant Road. I felt that I was not quite so committed. When the staff at the Deaconess Order asked if I would be available to move to Newcastle in 1972, I felt that it was right to do so. I agreed to go to Newcastle to see what the work involved and to speak with some of the people there.

In the meantime, it looked as though the Methodist Church was going to be able to pass a resolution at Conference in 1972, to admit women into the full-time ministry. If that was going to be so, I felt that that was a commitment I wanted to take. The Chairman of the Lincoln District at that time, Vincent Corner, thought that I ought not to take that step. He said that I was too valuable in the Wesley Deaconess Order and that the Order would need people such as myself. I had felt that from the beginning of my call, if it had been possible for me to be ordained to the ministry of the word and the sacrament, then that was my calling. I had talks with the Chairman to see whether it might be possible, at my age, to candidate for the ministry when that became possible, after the resolution had been passed. We began to look for my replacement in the LCCTM Someone would have to take over some of the work I had been doing in industry and in commercial chaplaincy. I also had to think about my own life and what it would be like to be in an entirely different kind of team. I had to prepare for another period of pioneering work.

Padley Chapel

There is a quiet here in these stone walls.
A peace wrested out of pain,
Conviction, loyalties – death.
The price paid, the conquerors live on.
The worship they prized
Continues – free.
The alter stone, the centre of
The sacrifice they claimed
And emulated, serves still
To you and me.
Would we so guard the privilege
To worship as we chose?
Enough to die for it?

Who knows?

9

Overseas Students in Newcastle
1972 - 1975

W E HAD an International House for overseas students in Newcastle. It catered for about fifty students and it was in the Jesmond area, on Osborne Road, next door to the Northumberland Hotel. The hotel management wanted to buy the International House and build an extension to the hotel. The committee, attached to the university, was ecumenical and met in Newcastle. They had decided to sell the House in order to fund a scheme to help overseas students on a broader basis because the Polytechnic in Newcastle was increasing rapidly. They were offering degrees in law and business management which were attracting more overseas students into Newcastle. They reckoned there would be more than six thousand overseas students studying there in the future. The committee wanted to prepare some sort of scheme that would help overseas students. That is what I went to do.

I went to see what the situation was and then to devise some scheme whereby we could offer help to overseas students on a wider scale and without any strings. They came from many countries and all kinds of religions and we could not make any distinctions. The Methodist Church would be serving on a broader scale. This was very much to my liking.

I went to meet the committee and to see if I was acceptable.

Obviously I was, much to my surprise, and then I was asked if I could go up to begin work in September 1971. I would look around, make my own decisions, and submit a plan. This I did. Dramatic days! There was no accommodation and no foundation. Everything was new and fluid. The committee was very helpful and at first I stayed in the YWCA, which was out at Jesmond. They were waiting for staff to come in. I think they were expecting a new deputy head, so I moved in to the very good accommodation prepared for her.

I began to visit the university, the chaplains, the other members of the team and the Polytechnic. I went to the Further Education Offices in Gateshead who catered for English and overseas students. I saw the officers who organised the accommodation. In fact, I did all the background work that was necessary. I agreed that we ought not to try to provide accommodation for overseas students as we had been doing in the International House. We needed to offer help on a wider scale. As I met some of the overseas students and the international group in the university, it seemed to me that a great deal of help was needed with study, visas and accommodation. Accommodation was a huge, open-ended problem: it was very limited and some was not suitable at all. There were a lot of landlords who only wanted overseas students for their money and then they provided them with very mean accommodation.

Looking around, I decided that we needed a centre, near to the University and the Polytechnic, which would be easily accessible to the overseas students from each venue. Probably we needed a kind of office where students could come to make their requests. Also, we needed a counselling room because it was evident that a great deal of counselling needed to be done. This was partly because the students had done their first degrees in the country of their origin. When they came to Newcastle they wanted to study for their masters degree, which meant they were in Newcastle for three or four years. The married students wanted their wives with them and this was a great problem to take on. Newcastle offered very good degrees.

A room was needed for some social activity. It had not to be too big, intimate enough for a family gathering and yet big enough for when we wanted to get varying country representatives together. We needed a place where there were instant coffee and tea making facilities. It had to be open to the students so that they could come and feel that they had a place of refuge.

I found offices in the middle of Newcastle. They were not very far from the YMCA which had more facilities should we need to work together. Finally, we decided to rent some premises on the ground floor of a big old house which was quite comforting to look at and a bit like home. They had been offices so there was a foyer with a great big counter, which gave privacy to the people behind it. There was a little office off this foyer, which was good for counselling. Behind that there was a large lounge with an open fireplace and a big window which looked out onto a small garden at the back. I felt that this was exactly the kind of place we were looking for.

There was a resident caretaker who had a flat on the top floor. She cleaned all the offices including ours. This meant that there was always someone there to contact and we did not require somebody else to be responsible all the time. That seemed to fit our need but we did have to furnish. We needed some easy chairs and a sofa or two in the lounge. We decided to have fitted carpeting throughout and to have some easy chairs in the offices. I had a 'whale of a time' going round Newcastle because it is a wonderful shopping centre. I loved finding the right curtains and carpets. I remember buying some chairs that seemed to me to be comfortable and yet small enough to allow us to accommodate more people. When they arrived they were all flat packs! They all had to be reconstructed! That made me think that we needed a lot of help. How were we going to staff all this? Who were we going to have in? I could not be there all of the time. I had other work to do. By that time, of course, all the fresher activities had begun and I had to be there to see how we welcomed overseas students. I had to get to know them and also to assess their needs because that was what I was there for. I began to ask around the committee and they helped. They manned the office and people came in to do all the bits of work. We asked our friends in the Circuit to look around for files, typewriters, office equipment, crockery – everything! It was pioneer work!

We had some really good times with that committee, looking ahead. Fortunately, as we had sold the International House, there was not a financial problem. They decided that the money was going to be spent on this new venture. That paid for my salary and gave us money to use for expenses. There was a lot of talent in Newcastle. There were a lot of people, for instance, who had worked abroad. There was also a great band of younger people, VSOs (Voluntary Service Overseas) who had perhaps spent two years in, say, Uganda and had a smattering of the language. That was very important. All these were exciting beginnings, getting people together and forming a team.

There was also another aspect of the work. I began to see that one of the needs was hospitality. We needed English homes where the family would welcome the overseas students and perhaps invite them to lunch on Sunday. That seemed to be a day when the students did not know what to do with themselves. Perhaps they could make a relationship with a family so that they could be invited out, perhaps for a weekend or an overnight stay sometimes. Hospitality had to be a kind of network all over the district and Newcastle was a large district.

I found a girl called Margaret Wingfield. It was a very strange thing. I had known her in Manchester and there she was in Newcastle. She came in to help me with hospitality. There was also a minister and his wife called Skidmore who were very helpful in hospitality. Actually, Margaret, after a few adventures finding my successor, took over from me. The work is still going on, though the office has been moved to another locality.

Another of the difficulties, I thought, was with the long-term students who wanted their wives to come over. Their wives often came straight from the extended family. What a culture shock! Finding suitable accommodation was a priority. So was helping them to fit into an entirely different way of life. Very few of them had any knowledge of English. It was no use sending them to Gateshead Further Education classes because they would have been no use to them. We had to begin simple English classes and we taught English by association: 'This is a cup and we drink from it'. 'This is a knife and we cut with it'. 'This is a chair and we sit in it'. When we came to describe chair legs we got into such a mess because legs have such a lot of connotations! But, it did seem to me that that was a very important thing to do. We had to be so careful with overseas students, any hint of patronage and they shied away. One had to be very careful how the helpers were chosen. They could not be 'do-gooders'. They had to be people who were genuinely interested in overseas work and liked the students for themselves and, if possible, knew a little about the country from which they came. This really became a big part of our work. We found teachers. Overseas students would be attracted to somebody who had been a teacher. We put them into groups and then they got to know each other. There would be two or three people, perhaps, of the same language and they would share.

Their dress! It was amazing really. I remember some students from Nigeria. They came from Kano and were sponsored by the Nigerian railways. Most of them studied business management. One lassie, whose name was Patti, came over and when she arrived in her first English grouping she was wearing a sarong and head-dress. Her hair was plaited in the theme of the family tribe and she was wearing a kind of flat sandal. Within a week, when Patti next came down to our groups, she was wearing a trouser suit, high-heeled shoes and a straight wig.

After the students had been in the English classes for some time, we thought that they were ready to go shopping or perhaps to do a bus trip. In this way, they would look at our coinage and see the value of their money. However, they came back confused and said that it was not English. It was the Geordie accent, of course, which made them think they were in a different country when they mixed with the population of Newcastle. Great hilarity!

Occasionally, Patti's husband had to go off to conferences and that left her a bit isolated and alone. Sometimes she would ask me to read his letters to her. It was quite amusing because he was her 'little puppy dog'. After a while Patti became pregnant and this was one of the difficulties we had to face because we were used to a good hospital background. We did not know that she was pregnant, just that she did not come to the classes. Most of the self-catering accommodation that people like that had, was in the west of Newcastle, not in the best areas. I decided I was going to see where Patti was. There was a house divided into 'bedsits'. I went up the stairs and found the number of the room. I knocked on the door but no one came, so I opened it and went in. It was in total darkness. There were electric fires blazing because of the cold. Then I saw, huddled on the settee in the darkness, this little figure in a sarong, bare feet – Patti!

I remember kneeling in front of her and saying, "Patti. Whatever is it? Are you ill?" She was not ill. "Why haven't you been coming?" She could not come. She thought she was expecting a baby!

"Have you told your husband?" "No. No!" You did not tell your husband. You told your mother-in-law and she told your husband. "Well, I'll have to be the mother in your family and I'll tell your husband!"

That is how it happened that I got her, with great difficulty, to go to the hospital. I only really persuaded her because I found her a Nigerian doctor who spoke her particular dialect of Hausa. Fortunately, his wife was expecting a baby too and that broke the ice. The doctor's wife got Patti to go to the clinics and have the examinations and made a friend of her. She did have her baby and it was a boy.

It really was a feature for a lot of our overseas students that husband and wife were apart for some of the time during pregnancies. Also, there were varying kinds of pregnancies according to the amount of money available. Some of our students, especially those from Iraq, were very rich and they could afford any kind of accommodation and every necessary help in pregnancies.

I always thought that the teaching of English was one of the best things that we did because we served our overseas students without patronising them. Part of our work was in the Chinese area where they were very poor but very, very keen to learn English. There were a lot of people who heard of our association English classes and wanted to join but we could not stretch our facilities. Our work was with the overseas students at the University and the Polytechnic and we had to help them. There was a man called Norman de Lacy who volunteered to come in to be a regular voluntary worker. He was a great help. He came in and I could trust him to receive the students. There was a woman, who came in from Hartburn, called Margaret Robson, whose son was a student at the University; also Miss Humphries and her sister, both ex-teachers. John Kilner was called in if there were any financial difficulties and there were many students with financial difficulties. There were helpers who had knowledge of work, for example applying for work visas, because that was also a great difficulty for the students. And personal difficulties arose because the overseas students found our society very free, especially association of females with males. It was a great temptation for them.

We had to learn about their basic cultures. We found out about the things that they liked to cook and to eat. Very often we had a supper arrangement where people brought in their favourite dishes, explained them and then we shared them. We, too, brought in our favourite dishes. Apple pie was their favourite English dish.

10

Candidating for the Ministry
at Newcastle
1973

W E COULD never serve sandwiches because the students would open them up to see what was inside them and, of course, the Muslims would not eat pork. We had to learn from our mistakes and get to know what they ate. Things like yoghurt and salads were usually universal and they liked that kind of thing.

The Thais had their own method of eating. When they invited us out, we learned how to eat their way. They had a circular table and everyone sat round it, looked at the food and picked up a little bit. If I picked up the wrong bit, quite often it tasted to me like rotten fish but it was a delicacy to them. It was a kind of learning process but such an exciting learning process.

I had to build up my files to keep a record of student needs, like the places from which they came and what they were doing in their studies. There was, for instance, a big group of nurses. One I remember in particular who trained as a nurse in Bangkok. All of the overseas nurses expected to come over and find a place here but the standard to which they had been trained was much lower than ours. It was more like St John's Ambulance standard and they did not realise that. There was also the language difficulty and that was true of our medical students. They could not go into the wards because they did not know enough English. If they tried to explain to the patients it was often a bizarre story of wrong captions, wrong prescriptions and wrong diseases. Some of the nurses came from Venezuela and they were used to working with children. They were longing to work with children again but they could not do so because it was too risky. These were all frustrations and we had to deal with them.

It was very difficult for an overseas student to prepare a thesis because the lecturers and tutors would speak too quickly. They forgot or did not even think that the overseas students were thinking in their own language and had to translate into English before they could write down what the tutor was saying. Some of our students would be accommodating enough to help with notes afterwards, but not many of them. The overseas students really worked. It was a tremendous privilege for them to be doing these courses. They were the leaders in their own country and they were being trained for leadership. They did not waste any time but our British students often treated the first year in university as a 'freedom flight' and did not work hard enough.

We had accountancy courses which took four years. If a student failed any of the examinations, he or she had to go back to the beginning and start again. When money was a problem, it was difficult. For instance, our students from Sierra Leone did not have any government grants but their families sponsored them privately. I remember Vicky who was doing accountancy. I think she had a small grant but gradually three brothers appeared. How they managed to get into this country I do not know because they did not have any money. They went to the house where Vicky had accommodation and they shared it. I dare not think how they shared. Their money used to come from their mother in dribs and drabs. Whenever I went there, they were using a great big stew pot with a kind of semolina in it and that was how they existed. They sat round it and dipped their fingers in the semolina. There did not seem to be any meat or anything else with it. When Vicky was approaching her fourth year, that was the end. A phone call came from Sierra Leone for her. It was the first time I had heard African wailing and it was because Vicky's mother had died. Without hesitation she said she had to go home. She had to find the first flight to take her back. We talked to her: "You can't go now, Vicky. That's giving away everything. You can't. You will have to start all over again. You are just at the edge of getting your qualification. That's what you have come to do. You want to be able to help when you return to your own country. You are a leader. You must not give it up."

Yes, she knew, but there was a great deal of corruption in Sierra Leone. The money that her mother sent came from little houses that she had in a compound. It was the rent they got from those little houses that was keeping her brothers. She had to go home because if she did not somebody else would steal the houses and the source of income would be lost. She had to go and she never came back. This was the kind of corruption that was operating in so many of those countries. We found this also in what we called our re-entry problems. When the overseas students had finished their degrees, quite often they were no longer acceptable in their own countries. This was despite their being sponsored by their governments to be trained as leaders. They went back with new ideas and broke the class system.

Another boy came from Sri Lanka. Wick was what we called him; his father owned a coconut plantation and his mother was a doctor. Wick did not approve of the way his father ran the plantation. We always suspected that there was an arranged marriage because he never wanted to go back to Sri Lanka. He kept doing other courses to keep him in the University teams. During one vacation he even joined a music group that toured Germany. Anything that prevented him from going back! He said that if he went back, he could not put into practise the kind of ideas he wanted to operate in Sri Lanka. Wick would have to go back into the same 'set'. He would only be acceptable in that 'set'. He made some associations with some of our English girls and we often wondered if he was free to do so.

When we went to Sri Lanka, I hoped that I could do some follow-up work. I kept in touch with some of the students particularly through Lance Robson, who was the secretary of the international committee. He kept in touch with people like Wick and Nurma, another of the boys from Sri Lanka. When I went to Sri Lanka, I wanted to look them up. Unfortunately it was at the time of the local elections and the president was assassinated. When I looked for Wick, I found out that his mother had had a surgery in Colombo. One day somebody had come into the surgery and shot her at point blank range. Wick had taken his father, left Sri Lanka and gone to America. Lance gave me his address in New York and I have since contacted him. He is working through the Internet. He has married a girl in New York who was also from Sri Lanka and has started a new life there. That is just a little window into some of the difficulties that our overseas students faced.

Something else I learned was never to trust completely the reports about overseas countries in the media. We would have headlines in all the newspapers and then we would meet someone from Sierra Leone or Vietnam (at that time) and they would say that the stories were not true. The events were not happening. They had heard that the reports were not right and they would be so indignant. So we learned not always to trust the media. Reporters can distort things sometimes. We could see how international incidents could ripen just because a word was translated incorrectly. The whole concept could be wrongly interpreted.

We learned so much about the whole world as our students came from so many countries. We learned about the kinds of culture. The Thai students, for instance, were so gentle and generous and hospitality in their country was very important. They gave up everything they had. If it was their last chicken running around, they killed it so that they could make a meal for a guest. We learned that we judge from our western perspectives and did not really understand the position in other countries.

We offered all kinds of help without any strings at all and so increasingly our centre became the advisory centre for overseas students. They told each other about it and if they needed help or if they needed to talk, I was a 'Mother in Israel' for so many of them because they confided in me. I think they found it easier to confide in a woman.

I had six hundred students on my files. They had been to us for help with things like work, accommodation and a lot of personal difficulties. They loved being in our country. That is why so many of them did all sorts of courses so that they did not have to go back. I often wish that I had accepted more of their invitations to visit their countries, particularly those from the people who were doing the medical courses. Newcastle specialised in neurology, which was something very important to them. The Iranian students were so cultured and had so much to give. I always think British people do not do enough talking and trying to understand overseas political situations. I know we tried to, because Newcastle became a great place.

The Polytechnic began to offer degree courses like the BA course for nursing students. They came out after five years with a management certificate and a BA degree. This caused a lot of consternation amongst our own nursing students who felt that those students had not done enough practical work and had not gone through the same traumas as 'our group'.

The African students sent back part of their grant to their families so that their younger brothers, not often their sisters, could be educated. They had to pay for their education. We do not appreciate the privileges enjoyed by our children.

While I was setting up our advisory centre and gathering together all our helpers, and terrific helpers they were, the hospitality work was also beginning to strengthen with great difficulty. Overseas students are not very good timekeepers. When our hosts had provided a lunch, with perhaps a Yorkshire pudding that had to be served exactly on time at, say, 2.30 in the afternoon, our students had not arrived. I would say that people had had a meal ready for them and that it was impolite not to be there on time. They would counter this by saying that in their country they could go and see their friends at midnight and they would still provide a meal for them. They were welcome at any time. They did not have to fit in to any kind of schedule. So they had difficulties in understanding our culture. However, the hospitality system really did help tremendously because when a student was invited into a British family he/she was taught language-wise, culture-wise, friendship-wise, sharing-wise, trouble-wise and joy-wise. Hospitality was really something we knew we had to build up gradually.

Bigger groups of students came to us in the 'fresher weeks' because we arranged special events for them. We had a lot of Spanish students who were very keen to learn English but at a higher level. They came in their own time which was usually about five o'clock and we met in the lounge. We just had an informal group and we brought in copies of *The Manchester Guardian* and *The Telegraph*. We would read, they would ask how we pronounced words and what they meant. That was a very different kind of teaching but it drew them all together. We continued to help them in these groups all through the summer and their vacations.

We also helped students with writing a thesis. They had great difficulty with translation of the language. They probably gathered all their information successfully but getting it down on paper, in the right sort of form, was a problem. Presentation was so important and often their presentation was poor. We set up a system where we had advisers who had done a thesis themselves. They knew what was expected in the way of margins and everything to do with presentation, including getting the thesis typed and all the things like that. Those were the days before you could call upon the computer. The typing was very important and so was the kind of paper on which it was presented. We helped them in all of these practical ways. I suppose the University and the

Polytechnic should have done that but they did not do it individually. I think that was the whole idea. It was the individual help which was so important.

There was another aspect of my time in Newcastle that I ought to mention here because it was part of my life. I had decided that if the Methodist Conference, which was at that time meeting in Newcastle, decided that the door should be opened to women in the ministry, then I would candidate, if I could be accepted. I reckon that I must have been sixty-two at that time. If I did not candidate then, that was the limit. I could not have candidated after that. I knew that I could not waste any time.

I am always grateful to John Mitchell who was in charge of the Westgate Church. It was a mission church helped by the Nixon family, who had set up a hospital in Sierra Leone. They were very missionary minded in a broad sort of way. John came to see me and said, "You know, I wonder if you would mind if your membership came to me, then you could come through our Circuit Meeting. You see, if you don't have a unanimous vote, I don't think you have much chance." Then he continued, "You know, Kenneth Waights, who is the Chairman of the District, will be on your side". There was also another fellow for me called Jim Bestford. He was an older minister and in charge of Local Preachers and Secretary of the Synod.

I will always remember when the result came through that Methodism had voted to allow women to train for the ministry. There were so many stipulations! Women had to go right back to the beginning and candidate again. They were not to be given any concessions. Women had to candidate under the same conditions as the men.

I had to go right back to the beginning. My Local Preacher's marks were looked at. I had to submit a book list, take trial sermons, do some study to prove that I could study. I had to appear before all the committees as well. Oh dear! I had to have a good health record. My heart sank – I thought I was not going to be able to do it! However, I did do all that.

I was looking up my diary because I was not sure that I had had a unanimous vote but I did. It was twenty-nine out of twenty-nine in the Westgate Circuit. I began to go to Westgate because I had to have a sponsor, a minister, and be under his care. John was my sponsor. I am eternally grateful to him.

So, at the same time as doing my job, I had to begin all the questionnaires, marks, book list and trial sermons. Two were delivered locally and one was a written sermon for the District Committee, all properly headed and presented. I went to Morpeth for one and I was so glad because Tom Earis was the minister. He had given me the opportunity to continue my ministry when I went home to look after Dad. Tom was there for the trial sermon with a supernumerary minister called Hall. The second trial sermon was at Alnmouth. That was a smaller church. The service was on a Thursday evening at seven o'clock and they were having a kind of supper. It was a fish supper and there were tables set out along each side of the hall. There was all this fishy smell coming off in between. I thought, "Oh dear! This isn't the right atmosphere!" However, it was all right. I think I got a two. I remember them saying to me afterwards that they thought it would be enough to get me through!

That was all going on in the background. Then there were all the district committees. It is a funny sort of feeling being questioned again when you have got beyond all that questioning: thinking about your theology, the things that matter most to you, the basic things you are going to preach. The question as to why I wanted to be in the ministry was hurled at me all the time. The committee members thought that I had a satisfying job and that I was good at my job. They did not understand why I wanted the ministry. I had to give my testimony and be accepted. Then I had to wait and see how many votes I had got. It was the full process.

I always think it was rather unfair that we had to wait in doubt. I have served on the Candidates' Committee since then and I realise that very early in the stages one was put into a category. One was an A, B or C student. If one was an

A student one did not really have much to worry about but I was never told that. I was always on tenterhooks until the results came through. I never knew. I remember walking along one of the streets in Newcastle and meeting a person who had been at Synod. He asked me if I wanted to know the result. I replied that I thought John Mitchell ought to tell me. He was the minister and my carer so I thought I would like him to tell me.

But you see, I had been an A student all the way along and I did not need to go through all that trauma. If they had just told me a little bit. ....Perhaps it is different now but it was very hard then.

The Vase

The vase was given to me
When my mother's great-aunt died.
Nearly 200 years old it must be-
Slender, silver-topped, glass feet tied.
Today it stands in the dappled sun
Holding in its slender care
Flowers of gentle colour
Singular and rare:
A soft blue daisy, a lily blushing red
And three pink chrysanthemums-
By clear, clean water fed.
Each day they stand serene and still,
A cluster of beauty – on the
Window sill.

– 11 –
The Call to Ministry in Lincoln
1975 - 1983

NOW I had another decision to make. I would have liked to go back to college. One of the things that I would have loved to do was to have had the opportunity for further study and to take a degree. The candidating committee, however, decided that as I was in a new job and already had a lot of experience, I could do my studying and internal training where I was, at the University of Newcastle. I did not have to make up my mind what to do straight away and I did not need to go to college.

The overseas students' committee was not at all sure about things. My salary as a deaconess was one thing, but if I were to be a minister they would have to find more money. They would have to provide a manse and follow all the rules and regulations. They were very disappointed when they found that I might be leaving. I decided that it was only honest to do so because that was what I wanted. I wanted to have the authorisation of the church that I was a minister of the word and the sacraments. Perhaps that really meant that I ought not to be in sector ministry. I always remember the committee sitting around as I made my decision. It was a bit like going back to Brimington, where they said that I had promised to leave my father and my mother. The committee asked me why I was leaving them just when all the work was really getting under way. Douglas Brown came down to see me because he was so impressed with the work at Newcastle. He thought it was the pattern that other International Houses ought to follow. He asked me to find the time to write it up as a pioneer experiment. He would publish it as a guide to other International Houses because they were all facing the same dilemma of more overseas students and how to look after them. That was never done. I did miss quite a number of opportunities.

We began to look for a successor. I remember Eddie Walton, the secretary of the committee, who was the prime mover behind all of this, being very upset about it. He thought I was the right person and that they did not want me to leave. He and the committee could not face all the upheaval. He reminded me that I had got my flat and that he had furnished it. But then he relented and said that it had to be my decision. Eddie was not happy about it but I reassured him and told him not to worry about it. The organisation that we had set up would run for two years but after that they would need to be looking for new directions. He reminded me about that many times because that is how it happened. Fortunately, before I moved, Margaret Wingfield had become my assistant because she had handed over the hospitality to the Skidmores. By that time most of our group committees had been set up and were running. Some time after I had left Margaret came in and took over. She had been in from the beginning and had been trained by me. She followed the same lines and saved the whole system.

Jim Bestford suggested that I could find an appointment in Newcastle and then I could keep 'an eye on things'. I did not know how I was going to do that. I went down to South Shields to look at three churches. I was supposed to look after three churches and also keep 'an eye' on the overseas students' work. It was a bit much to ask. I decided to leave Newcastle and then the invitations started to come in.

An invitation came in from Lincoln. I was to be the second minister in the South Circuit which was quite a big step forward. I had expected to have to stay somewhere down on the bottom rung of the ladder but this was quite a long way up the ladder. It was Alan Dye's doing. I knew Alan, of course. I knew the Circuit. I was coming back into the Circuit where I had done my first Local Preaching. My recognition service as a Local Preacher was held at St. Catherine's Church. In many ways this was a very attractive prospect particularly as the manse was in Hykeham and Fred was not very far away. I could let him keep his independence and I mine, but keep in touch all the time, without too much travelling. Geoff was also in Hykeham at that time so that seemed to be right. Geoff and Joan moved to Skellingthorpe on 20th March 1978.

It was a big venture. I had seven churches: Swallowbeck, Moor Lane, Hykeham village, Aubourn, Bassingham, Carlton and Brant Broughton, where I also became the chairman of the school governors. I did not know that then. I only knew that it was the right invitation to accept, if I was acceptable to them. They had knowledge of me and I had knowledge of them. It seemed right all round. St Catherine's Church was still the main church of the Circuit at that time. Then began all the folding up of work, all the sad farewells and handing over.

I want to say something here about accommodation because in the Deaconess Order it was always a bit of a thorny problem. I think that it needs to be talked about. When I went to Liverpool there was no accommodation for me. I lived out of a suitcase and moved from place to place when people came home from the war. There was no flat. There never was. It was the same in Newcastle. I stayed at the YWCA for a time and then I moved to the Dene Hotel. I rather liked that. They were a nice group of people. They were mostly representatives. One thing I did not like about it was that we had meals round one big table. Sometimes I only had breakfast but usually I had an evening meal as well.

We were looking for a house, at first, when we began looking for accommodation but that did not prove to be practical, so we decided upon a flat in the centre of Newcastle in Berwick Court. We did this because we could look out over the advisory centre which was 3 Ellison Place. I could see the centre from my bedroom window. It was on the eighteenth floor. I had never really lived in a flat before but I could see the Tyne from my window and the ships coming up the river. There were two lifts, one for even numbers and one for odd numbers. Often the lifts were out of order and I was terrified of being caught in the lift halfway with the alarm buttons not working. Also, it was a bit scary because we never knew who was living in such a big block of flats. We had doors with little spy holes so that we could look out and see who was there.

The interesting thing was that it was entirely unfurnished so I had the next exciting experience of buying everything: carpets, curtains, suite, dining table, four chairs, sideboard, lamps, kitchen and bedroom equipment, beds, and a wardrobe which could second as a desk. That really became a home for me. It was wonderful because it was so near the University and the Polytechnic.

I had my membership at Central Methodist Church. That was a very welcoming and warm church. I preached there often but I preached all round the District because they wanted to know about the Centre. I used my Mini. There was no garage at first so I kept it at the United Reformed Church when I went to the offices. The URC was built on some land where houses were being demolished. Once I went away on holiday and when I came back a trench had been dug. There was my little Mini sitting on an island with a trench all round it! The workmen had to put planks across this trench so that I could get my little car out. In the building where I lived there was basement accommodation for parking. When Margaret took over, she did not need it because she lived in Sunnyside. I do not know what happened to all my lovely furniture and things. They were just absorbed or sold, I think. However, that home is no longer.

Unfortunately, I candidated and decided to come to

Lincoln at the time when ministers were given the privilege of buying their own furniture. I had to leave my furnished flat in Newcastle for my successor, so I did not have any furniture. The furniture in Newcastle belonged to the Centre. When I came to Lincoln, Margaret and her husband brought me. He put all that I had in a trailer at the back of the car. My books were to come on later. When we went into the manse, the only furniture was a table with four chairs in the dining room, which was a long room, and one bed in the main bedroom.

Thankfully, I had left some furniture at home: books, a divan bed, an armchair and a desk. These were the things which I had never moved to Newcastle. They had been moved to Fred's and were still there so I knew that I had some basic furniture. The carpets were in a dreadful condition. Some were in holes. Some of the curtains had great big sunflowers on them and were brown. I was rather dismayed because I would have to start again with bills. I could not afford furniture. Somebody told me about a place 'up hill,' just round the corner from here. They had very good quality furniture. My friend advised me to go and have a look. I had found out that there were bookings of special preachers coming to the Circuit and I was supposed to give them accommodation. That seemed to be what happened in the Circuit. The second minister provided accommodation and – well – only one bed! I furnished the manse with second hand furniture for about £180, or something like that, because I did not have any money. I really did love having my own manse, but that is a different story.

Lincoln and the 'A B C run'
1975 - 1983 cont.

MARGARET Wingfield, who helped me in the centre in Newcastle and her husband Maurice brought me down to Lincoln. We found a stove which George Malton had stored in his garage. It was an old English Electric stove. It was installed in the manse. The Circuit Stewards said that there would be the possibility of having different curtains. There would perhaps be some new carpets as well but I expected that that would be in the future. I began to unpack my books in the study and make that my own. Fred brought over my furniture in his pickup. About September 6th, Fred and Geoff installed my television and then I began to feel at home.

I started preaching in the Circuit on September 7th. There was a service at Swallowbeck on that Sunday morning, at 10.45 and a Circuit Service at night. I had been invited to preach at both of those services. I was very impressed with Swallowbeck. There was a good congregation and a lot of young people. That gladdened my heart. My pastoral charge was for seven churches. Swallowbeck was the main church. Moor Lane Church was along Moor Lane in North Hykeham. Hykeham Village Church was a little church right in the crook of the village near the shops. Next there were Auburn, Bassingham, Carlton le Moorland and Brant

Broughton, which also had an Anglican/Methodist Church school.

There was the Chairman's reception and my induction service at St. Catherine's Church on September 11th. It was absolutely packed. The entire gallery was full. The subject of my address was 'Coming in full circle' because it was at St. Catherine's that I had preached my Local Peacher's trial sermon and had my recognition service as a Local Preacher.

The visiting began because people were ill and I was the minister. I had left my little Mini at Fred's home in Brant Road so I went to collect it. The gas, electricity and all the other services were connected. I followed Revd Alan Dye and his wife. I did think that perhaps, as I was a single minister, people would feel they were missing out because there was nobody at the manse when I was out visiting and working. But I found that when I asked people to ring me early in the morning, it worked very well. Actually, since Alan's wife taught and the children were at school and Alan often acted as chauffeur to one or other of them, I was often at the manse more than they had been, especially in the mornings.

People began to visit me and one of them was the Anglican vicar, Revd Andrew Bennett. I understood that he was not really looking forward to working with a woman. When he came to see me, I told him that I understood he was not very keen on having a woman as a colleague. He replied that I was much more Anglican than he thought I would be. Actually, we had a very good relationship and worked together ecumenically. One of the joys I had was taking evensong in the parish church; I loved the corporate worship and the spontaneity of the responses.

My ministry in the Lincoln South Circuit began. The Superintendent was Paul Jefferies from St. Catherine's Church and my colleagues were David Wolf at Moorland Park and a curate called Terry Stokes. We had our first staff meeting which served to introduce me to a lot of my colleagues. I went to the crematorium and learnt all about funerals. The administering of the sacraments, funerals and marriages were part of my pastoral charge and I was not very familiar with any of them. Then the hospital visiting began. I remember going up to St. George's Hospital to see somebody there. All these experiences were very enriching and took place quite soon after my arrival.

One of the things that gave me great joy was that on September 12th I had a visit from Margaret Harrison. I had known Margaret in my Manchester days because she was the secretary of the Nurses' Christian Movement. She had met a medical student at that time called Donald Harrison. Margaret had intended going out somewhere as a missionary after finishing her nursing training but when she met Donald they fell in love and they were married. To my surprise, they had a medical practice in North Hykeham. It was really lovely to find people who had known me in Manchester and now we could do some work together in this new appointment.

The preaching plan had already been made and so I found myself planned at Hykeham village and then out at Aubourn. Moor Lane had a much younger and outgoing congregation. They had started a successful mums' and toddlers' club. Hykeham Village Church had a more elderly congregation but a very good youth club. They turned one of the outhouses into a sort of 'cellar' where the youth club met. Alwyn Warnes led the club. He was the youth leader and was a teacher at the North Kesteven School. He was also a Local Preacher and a great help in the village church.

I had a chaplaincy at Fosse House in North Hykeham. This was a residential home for the elderly run by Lincoln Council. I held a service there on a Thursday morning and Mrs Fox was the pianist. One of the people who was often in charge at Fosse House was Mrs Couchman who was a member at Swallowbeck

I found the shopping centre – a very lively place called The Forum. It was not far away from the manse. I discovered that I had another colleague, from the Central Circuit living at 41 Harewood Crescent. I was at No 12. The St Hugh's Church, which was Anglican, was also in Harewood Crescent. Terry Stokes, the curate, was nearby, and opposite was the area secretary of the NSPCC so our crescent was really a 'holy club'.

Tony Needham and his wife Marylin were some of the first people to come and see if they could help. Tony came to cut the lawns. They were both very friendly and had two small children, Tracey and Lisa. They lived in St. Aiden's housing estate off the Newark Road. Quite a lot of people who came to Moor Lane lived on that new estate. Swallowbeck had a lot of youth organisations such as Brownies, Guides and toddlers' clubs. Since they all met on the premises, I was the unofficial chaplain to them all. There was also a youth officer, who worked in our Circuit, Colin Ride, and he was very helpful in telling me about the youth work in the Circuit. I valued his colleagueship very much.

Aubourn Methodist Church was a lovely little church. It was a replacement for an older church which had to be pulled down. Mr and Mrs Frank Taylor lived in Aubourn and Mrs Taylor was determined that there should still be a Methodist church there. She found the money in varying ways to build the church. I think that it cost about £1,000. They were the 'moving lights'. We also had some Local Preachers who lived there, including Mr and Mrs Percy Norman. There were several people there who were very loyal to the church. The church and the surroundings were beautifully kept.

There was a Circuit service at Aubourn every Good Friday in the afternoon, followed by a tea in the village hall. This was a wooden hut and there were long tables set out for the congregation. After tea, there were walks to find both purple and white violets. The paths went by the old mill and ancient Anglican church. Violets could be found by the river and under the hedges. The walkers arrived back at the Methodist church in time for a service of song at six o'clock. Very often the choir sang a cantata such as 'Olivet to Calvary' to complete the Good Friday devotion.

The next church along, in what we called the A-B-C run,

was Bassingham. The church there was very big and seated six hundred people. It had a caretaker's house in the grounds and also a large building with a sloping floor. It had once been the Methodist Day School. Bassingham had some very good caretakers, the Hardys, who looked after the church and all the premises. They really were very loyal. The steward, Bassingham's funeral director, was called Ash. Then there was Helen, a 'live wire,' and one of the younger people living there. Also the Battersbys were old established members of the church.

Bassingham had a good Sunday School. It had one of the 'old-fashioned' Sunday School anniversaries with special hymns and the choir practised for weeks beforehand. All the people took part with a variety of recitations, readings and songs. On the day after the anniversary, which was usually in June, all the children met together. The farmers brought their tractors and trailers with little harmoniums which we put on the trailers along with all the children. We went round the villages and they sang the anniversary songs. I think that it was one of those practices which are rapidly dying out in the country. I got the television people down to take recordings of them. When we came back from singing round the villages we had tea which was provided in the large schoolroom. It was a kind of 'bean feast' with sports afterwards. Those anniversaries and getting ready for them were very happy times. As had been the custom for many years, people came from other churches round about and from the Circuit to take part in them. People invited other people to tea and it really was a happy celebration to be remembered.

Bassingham was an important part of my ministry. We had a family service there once a month at ten o'clock. Often I would go to Bassingham for that service and then on to Brant Broughton for a service at eleven. Bassingham had a very good school. They had rebuilt the school and incorporated it into the village hall and playing fields. It became quite a social centre. Some good things were done there and it was a growing village.

My next church was Carlton le Moorland. It was a small village church in which Mr and Mrs Bell played a leading role. Mr Bell was a great singer with a good voice and he led the singing. There was a hand-pumped organ and he pumped it while his daughter played. I have very warm memories of Carlton le Moorland because of the intimacy and warmth of the services. This was a farming area and the people who were Methodists in the farming community were the Waltons. I remember thinking I would go on to Carlton le Moorland one night to do some visiting and to get to know the people. I entirely forgot that in the village, at that time, there would be no streetlights and it was in absolute darkness. I realised that in the dark I could not find my way to any of the addresses on my list!

Next came Brant Broughton, another church in my charge. It was a large church and the seats were arranged in a circular fashion. Attached to it there was another large building which was the Methodist Day School. It was really on an island and behind it was Clegg's field. I became the Chairman of the Governors and it was an interesting committee. This was at the beginning of having parents on the Board of Governors. At the time pupil numbers in rural schools were being questioned. The school was 130 years old. I remember the headmistress doing a pageant through the years with all the children taking part. The girls were in little white pinafores with white bob caps carrying their slates and slate pencils. They had all their lessons in one class for the pageant and not divided up into several classes as we do today.

There was also a Church of England Junior School in the village and our school was in question. If our numbers fell below thirty, we were in danger of being closed. We decided to fight this closure and we certainly did. I remember exciting meetings and in the end we won. It really was because we had Clegg's field. It was decided finally that we would build a new school on Clegg's field and that this would take up to a hundred children. We would accommodate both our school and the Church of England school. Both of them would close and then amalgamate in one new Anglican / Methodist School. Perhaps there would also be accommodation for other children, probably from Stapleford and perhaps Carlton le Moorland.

Brant Broughton is a very lovely village with a lot of beautiful old houses. The Anglican Church is really famous because of the frescos which were found on the altar. They are part of a set of four and very valuable indeed. The Wesleyan Reformed Church, which was very independent, had its headquarters in Ruskington and never really joined with us much. We had our harvest thanksgiving together with the Anglican Church in alternate years and we always had the remembrance service together.

We took out the centre pews in the church and carpeted it and then we were able to have choirs and concerts which were very well attended. It was very successful because there was a good organ at Brant Broughton. We decided that we would have the church decorated and that was a big task because it was so high. All the windows needed repairing but we really wanted to make it beautiful, which we did. Unfortunately, while we were doing the high ceiling, the scaffolding fell onto the organ and damaged the pipes so we had to have that repaired as well. Fortunately, it was covered by insurance. The firm called Jubbs came to do the repair.

Also in Brant Broughton there was the Friends' Meeting House. Its history went back to 1642. It was really two cottages. Where we entered, there was still the old range and brick oven. It was a very simple white meeting-house with all the forms set round a central table. In the entrance, there was an old mounting stone from the days when people came on horseback. The stables were at the back of the house. To the left there was the huge shed where the traps were kept. People came in by horse and trap to worship. Behind the stables was a quiet burial place where many of the family of Burts were buried. Burts were big farmers in the area and still are. They have been Quakers for generations. They kept the Meeting House going. It is a very quiet and beautiful little place built on Meeting House Lane. The Brant Broughton congregation was never large in numbers but I always felt it was worthwhile. The Brownlows and the Becketts were the people at the heart of it and kept it going.

Those, then, were my churches and I was very fond of them.

– 13 –
Lincoln and then – Retirement?
1983

TAKING funerals, especially at the crematorium, was both sad and joyful- yet at the same time interesting and good for me because they were family occasions. I got to know the officials and became part of the team. The man who was largely responsible for the burial grounds was Edward Richards and he was married to Maisie. I had known Maisie in my Nottingham days when I was a deaconess there and she was a nurse at the General Hospital. We had kept in touch, rather loosely, but it was lovely to know that they were in Lincoln and living in the Newport Lodge. Maisie was working at the Bromhead Hospital in the maternity section. There were two other hospitals in Lincoln. I liked St George's Hospital. It was warm and friendly and a lot of our people went into St. George's rather than the County Hospital.

I preached around the Circuit and that was interesting because when I said I had come full circle coming to the South Circuit, that was really so. As a young Local Preacher I had preached at St Catherine's, Moorland Park and some of the villages. In fact I was told I had preached one of my first sermons at Aubourn. I think it lasted about ten minutes! So I really had come back into familiar territory.

We gradually came to know our teams and learned how we could work together in our church councils. At Swallowbeck there was also the church family committee consisting of a representative from each organisation. Sandra and David Clack were the people who ran the youth work at Swallowbeck and Margaret Harrison began a club at Moor Lane. Alwyn Warnes ran the youth work at Hykeham village. There was no Sunday School at Carlton le Moorland. Youth work was very important in the Lincoln South Circuit and also played an important part in the whole of the area, having some connections with the Central Methodist Church. I also went out to preach at Birchwood and that was interesting to see how the new church had been progressing since my initial work.

There was another chore which had not been mine before. I had to find material and do a letter for two magazines. One was called *The Outlook* the magazine for Swallowbeck Methodist Church. All the different groups submitted articles and made it very interesting. There was a team of magazine distributors who were also news gatherers and pastoral visitors. This was a very efficient way of keeping in touch with our church family. The other magazine was called *The Link* and it was for Hykeham Village churches and the villages beyond. Our village churches shared pastoral care with the vicar there. He had Bassingham, Carlton and Aubourn so our 'Link' was interchangeable. We worked together. Copy was collected together in Hykeham and the vicar and I were editors.

An annual responsibility was the writing of class tickets/ membership cards, for the members of all seven churches. They were given out at the Covenant services which took place on the first and second Sundays in January, as is Methodist usage. I also ran membership classes. There were people in training for membership in all of my churches. It was a great privilege, especially bringing into membership the younger people.

There was work among the elderly. The women's meetings were mostly older people and there were social clubs in Bassingham and Hykeham, where I was expected to speak occasionally. In North Hykeham there was a very interesting experiment, mostly organised by Margaret Harrison. It was a pleasure to be able to work with her. At ten o'clock on a Wednesday morning, a bus went out to collect retired people which brought them to the Sports Centre, where a lunch was arranged. The Centre was part of the North Kesteven School. Afterwards there were varying activities and different people came in to speak. About three o'clock they were taken home again. It was a very good venture because it brought the older people onto the Sports Centre for a social occasion. There was a good swimming pool, so a lot of our people learned to swim, even at eighty years of age. Some people began to swim for the very first time. It was a very exciting, worthwhile venture for the older people in North Hykeham.

With seven churches to look after and seven church councils to lead, where there was a lot of discussion about property and finance, I was kept busy. Much of my work was taken up with funerals, baptisms and weddings and there was hardly a week without some preparation, some weddings or a funeral.

In 1980 a very exciting event took place at Swallowbeck. There had been a separate hut at the back of Swallowbeck. We had to go out of the main church to get to it. On the side of the hut there was a separate door. Most of our youth activities and a lot of our organisations met there. It had always been the hope that the main church might be extended so that this part of our premises might be part of the whole. We decided that we would go ahead with this venture and so we did. We had a very good committee going through all the preliminaries and the new church hall extension was officially opened on 6th September 1980.

Another important part of my work was in the schools. I can particularly remember working with the fourth year students in both North Kesteven and Robert Pattison Schools. It was mostly in the form of question and answer type forums. I also took assemblies in the Ancaster School with the local Anglican and Roman Catholic men in charge. We three gave a series of talks to the students there on family life, marriage and our church services. We found that with our baptism, marriage and funeral services all being modernised, there really was not very much difference except in the wording here and there. This helped to bring our churches together.

There was a lot of preparation work to be done. There were three, sometimes four, services on a Sunday including family services which took more preparation. There were anniversaries and special services, such as weddings, where one had to prepare an address. Although this meant a lot of work, it gave me much pleasure. The manse was a centre for hospitality. If we had people to take a special service then they spent the weekend, usually, at the manse.

The time came for a new car because of travelling through the area. It was a new Mini 1000. I covered many miles: Swallowbeck, the Hykehams, then out to Aubourn, Bassingham, Carlton and Brant Broughton, for the round trip, as well as visiting in the wider surrounding area. It was not only the Sundays but other days of the week as well. The work in the Lincoln South Circuit was very satisfying for me. I had wondered, when I was in Newcastle, whether it was right for me to come into Circuit work, but it certainly was. I felt that I had the authority now to administer the sacraments. The taking of baptisms, being the authorised person for weddings and the taking of funerals, bound us together in a great family in our section, sharing our sorrows and our joys.

In spite of such a busy life it was possible to spend time with friends during these years. Since the Newcastle days, I had been a member of the committee for the oversight of probationers. This met regularly in London. I had enjoyed getting the 7.25am executive train from Newcastle, going straight down to King's Cross and then doing a bit of window shopping in Oxford Street before going on to Westminster Central Hall, where the committee met. I continued to be a member of that committee when I was serving in the Lincoln South Circuit. It gave me the opportunity of going quite regularly to London where I had a friend, Eileen Johnson. I met her when she was a student nurse in Nottingham and I had kept in touch with her. At that time she was the nursing officer for Barnett and had a flat over the Westminster Bank in Golders Green. It was very accessible. I often went to stay with Eileen and she came to stay with me. She would sometimes ring up on a Friday night, perhaps even at midnight and say that she had to get out of London and that she was coming there and then. She would stay for the weekend and then travel back. We had many happy holidays together. One of the most painful things I have ever done was to take Eileen's funeral. She had been taking a course for people about to retire in a local factory. She must have had a stroke because she pulled her car to the side of the road on her return journey from the factory and slumped over the wheel. A man found her and she was taken to hospital but she never recovered consciousness. I went to take her funeral which was held at our Methodist Church at Finchley and the crematorium at Golders Green. That was a very sad and exacting task for me.

I was not very far from Nottingham where I had another friend, Phil Elson. She had become a member of the church while I was a deaconess in Nottingham Mission. I had kept in touch with her and her brother Lionel who was an architect. Phil had been in the National Children's Homes and she trained as a sister there. She left her job in Nottingham to do that, but when her mother and father were ill she had to come back to Nottingham to nurse them. When they died, she and her brother Lionel shared a house which Lionel had planned and built. It was easy on days off to get to Nottingham and Phil often came to see me. It was really lovely having a manse big enough to offer hospitality to my friends. We had many lovely holidays together abroad because Phil and Lionel had travelled a lot and she had a lot of knowledge and helped me when I began to travel abroad.

I had another friend who was in college with me, Kathleen Marsh, who lived in Birmingham. She had gone out to marry Richard Marsh in the West Indies but after a while she developed thyroid trouble and they had to come back to this country. He was in the ministry in Birmingham. Unfortunately, he developed Parkinson's Disease and, though Kathleen was able to help him through the latter years of his ministry, in the end he died. Kathleen continued to live in Birmingham. I often went over to see her and she came over to see me.

It was lovely to have my brother Geoff and his wife Joan in Skellingthorpe and also to share their family of John and Heather. Margaret and Donald Harrison had been my friends in Manchester. We worked together on lots of ventures. In fact, although Margaret was brought up as an Anglican, she began to be interested in Local Preaching and came into membership at Moor Lane. She did her Local Preachers' examinations and in the end did the EMTEC (East Midlands Theological Ecumenical Course) course and is now an ordained minister. When they left Hykeham she worked in the Gainsborough Circuit. Now they have both retired and they live at Willoughby near Alford. Margaret does some work now in the Alford Circuit.

I had very good colleagues in Lincoln South Circuit. Paul Jefferies and David Wolf were part of the staff when I arrived. When Paul left we had Frank Smith who moved into a manse near Moorland Park. He and his wife became good colleagues. When John Warren was at Moorland Park he was a great help and we found we could diffuse Methodism with great pleasure. Eddie Greatham came as a supernumerary minister with his wife Rosemary. They came to live in Hykeham where they did some work together. Gordon and Doreen Scott were supernumeraries too, also living in Hykeham. Unfortunately, Doreen developed a brain tumour. They had two daughters, Rosemary and Margaret. It was a lovely family. Doreen died quite suddenly and Gordon was left alone. He had the support of his daughters who came to be with him as often as they could. Sadly, Gordon died and we felt the loss very much indeed.

We had good working relationships with the Anglicans,

Terry Stokes and Andrew Bennett, with whom we did a lot of ecumenical work. Ian Williamson had come to be the minister at the Central Church in Lincoln and they were in the manse in Harewood Crescent. There was a lot of warm fellowship and sharing around. There was good 'Fellowship of the Kingdom' in our area – a study group for ministers. We had a study paper which was issued every autumn and it brought us all together on a deeper level.

In 1981 thoughts of retirement began to creep in. I began to feel that having been six years in the Lincoln South Circuit, perhaps I ought to be looking elsewhere. Then I thought, well, perhaps it was time I retired! I had a talk with my Superintendent and with Eric Jones, who was the Chairman of the District at that time. They did not think it was time for me to go. I sometimes wondered, afterwards, whether I made the right decision but, since they all seemed to want me to stay, all the stewards had been interviewed and wanted that, I said I would stay for another two years and so I did. I continued working in the Lincoln South Circuit until 1983.

I began the series of preparations for moving out which perhaps only Methodism knows all about! There were invitations to ministers – people coming to be interviewed, people looking at the manse and at the churches and wondering if this was the place for them or not. Swallowbeck had in mind a man who had worked in Gainsborough. He was a friend of one of our families and he was leaving Gainsborough. He had preached at Swallowbeck and they had liked him. His name was Richard Temple and he was invited to follow me. There were all the farewells with all the organisations. It was very painful but in some ways very rewarding. I began to see the pattern my ministry had been weaving through eight years. Also, I reaped a little bit of the harvest I had been sowing diligently and hopefully, without always seeing the results I had expected.

Now there was the great question of what to do in retirement. I had been in the Lincoln District for a long time and I felt that I ought to move out of the Lincoln area to give my successor a clear field. For a time, I contemplated an invitation to Church Stretton but that was a very wide flung Circuit, forty miles to some appointments and along very busy roads. When ministers retire they can apply for a home to be provided by the Methodist Ministers' Housing Association (MMHA). I thought that perhaps something could be done for me. I went to London where I was interviewed by the Secretary of the MMHA and they offered me a bungalow in Caythorpe. However, the Methodist Church in Caythorpe had closed and I felt that that was not the place for me.

While I was debating what I should do, Dorothy Wells, whom I had known for some time in the Newark Circuit, contacted me. She was the Circuit Steward and she asked me if I would be interested in going into the Newark Circuit even though no manse was available. There was a supernumerary minister working in Collingham in his retirement. When we were in Norton Disney I had got to know Newark very well and I liked it. It was attractive because it was just over the border from the Lincoln District.

Swinderby, a little village near to Collingham is in the Lincoln District and Collingham is in the Nottingham and Derby District. It was not very far from Fred, which meant that I could go over through the back ways. I went round by Haddington, Aubourn, down Meadow Lane and into Brant Road to see him without going through the city. I could use my car. Also, Geoff and Joan were in Skellingthorpe and that was within easy distance of Collingham. Dorothy Wells said she thought the MMHA sometimes bought a property, if the minister thought it was the right place to go for retirement. We contacted them to see if they would do it. After a lot of delay, they decided that they would find £19,000. This would be for a small bungalow for a single minister like me, if such a property could be found in Collingham for that sum. There were some bungalows which had been built about 1980. We went to have a look and found that they did come within the price limit but the one that was empty had already been promised. In the next row there was a bungalow which was empty but it was £24,000. If I contemplated going into that bungalow then I would have to find the difference. That would be at least £3,000 out of my own money. The rules of the MMHA said that if I did pay money out of my own funds it could never be refunded. It was ranked as a donation to the MMHA.

I went to have a look at the bungalow again. I decided that perhaps it was worth consideration. Collingham was in such a good position for me and it was a village that had a community where one could feel at home. Perhaps I ought to do it. I decided on the bungalow which was 7 Monkwood Close in Collingham. It was ranked as a three bedroomed bungalow. The MMHA did not think I needed three bedrooms but one was very small and of the other two, one was quite roomy and the other was not. It was a nice bungalow and it was about fifteen minutes walk from the High Street and the Methodist Church in Collingham. Negotiations for its purchase began. Then came the farewells at Swallowbeck and I left the Lincoln South Circuit in August, 1983. I moved into the bungalow on 18th August.

In Awe

Every leaf on every tree is still
As if held by an unseen hand.
No bird song.
No sound breaks the silence in the land.
The skies are sullen, like a dark shelter for the earth.
No stars or moon - 'Tis night....
Is it nature's sleep...before
The magic of God's wand
Brings the awakening dawn
And light.

– 14 –
Collingham
1983

REVD Ron Hockney, Superintendent of the Newark Circuit, and Dorothy Wells, who was the Circuit Steward at that time, had come to see if I could do some work in Collingham. This was because Revd Bob Pridmore had died suddenly. Naturally, I said that I was willing to do whatever I could. I returned to the manse. Barnes Removals moved my furniture and John Turner came over to fix my fridge and my stove. Geoff, Joan and Fred came to help unpack. I stayed at Fred's for a few days. On August 27th Donald, Margaret and I went to Wales for a holiday in Llangollen, Anglesea, Holyhead, Beaumaris, Blackrock and Portmeirion where we saw the slate quarries. We visited some of Margaret and Donald's friends before returning on September 3rd. I discovered I was planned to preach at Collingham on September 4th. My ministry in Collingham began.

A deaconess had been coming over to Collingham for two days every week. Marjorie Bates had been stationed in Newark and was in the Newark Circuit. After Bob died, she had given pastoral care to the people of Collingham. My colleagues were Revd Ron Hockney, Superintendent, Revd Middlemiss at Southwell, Revd Richard Bielby in charge of Balderton, and a deaconess, Sister Dorothy Taylor, was in charge of our Hawtonville Church, which was on a new housing estate. Collingham also had an Anglican Church, where Canon Stephens had been the vicar for twenty-eight years. There were two Anglican Churches: St John the Baptist at South Collingham and All Saints at North Collingham. Archdeacon Woodham and Canon Ken Wright also helped in those two churches. Tony Suter was the Circuit Steward at that time and also there were my own stewards in the Collingham Methodist Church. They were my colleagues and the team with whom we worked. Mary Nicholson had drawn a map of Collingham for my use, with a list of members and a list of those on the community roll. There was also a list of the officers of the church and all of this was very helpful. In fact it was a great team to work with. Revd Brian Greet was the Chairman of the District and I had known him before. I moved into a warm, hospitable team of colleagues.

I took the harvest service on September 25th and at that morning service, which was a full house, there was a baptism, Ian James Huckaby. That seemed to set the scene for our family togetherness. It was the first baptism in my time at Collingham. Then I found that we had the privilege of going in to take assemblies at the John Blow Primary School. This school had about a hundred pupils and it was wonderful to be put in touch with all our younger members and to meet their families. The premises were good: the hall, the Wesley Hall, had once been the Methodist day school and it had a very good playgroup. We were in the community and this put us in touch with young families again. We began a Shell group which was a weeknight activity for the 'Young Church', as we called our Sunday School. There was also a very lively Guild. I went back to take their anniversary when the Guild had been operating for ninety years. The Women's Fellowship was an older group but a very warm fellowship. It was very outgoing in its thinking and with splendid officers. They kept a high standard in the programme, which was submitted for the whole year. The stage was set for a very good ministry.

There was a very enthusiastic MAYC group together with North Scarle under the leadership, at the beginning, of Alwyn Warnes. They took part in the Methodist Association of Youth Clubs' weekends and it was my privilege to join them there. A wonderful atmosphere was created in the London weekends and seeing all those thousands of youngsters gathering together in the Albert Hall made me feel proud of the Methodist Church.

The magazine called *The Fleet*, was named after a small river that runs through Collingham. It was an ecumenical magazine and had contributions from all denominations, led by an ecumenical group of the Collingham Council of Churches. It was really very lively. We all worked together on a variety of projects such as Christian Aid Week, Armistice Sunday and the Week of Prayer for Unity. This was valuable in a place like Collingham because the churches were seen to be working together. It was a most satisfying experience. As I got to know the people by daily visitation, I realised what a privilege it was to be the minister there and to have pastoral care of that Methodist Church, which was the hub of the community. The work began and continued because my ministry stretched over thirteen years.

One of the occasions I particularly enjoyed was the Nottinghamshire Show which was held in Newark. We always had a church tent with a bookstall and helpers served cups of tea. People from all over came to the Show and we made many contacts. In fact, it was almost like industrial chaplaincy all over again! It was during this time, when I was in Collingham in 1989, that the Methodist church decided that they would have a big study conference of churches in Malta. I was fortunate enough to be one of those selected as a representative in February that year. It was a great honour.

There were many developments in Collingham. I came to know most of the community. I realise what a trust it was to have entry into the homes and to be welcomed there. It was a privilege to take part in the joys and sorrows of the community. Baptisms, preparation for membership, confirmation services, weddings and funerals all bound us together with the silken cords of love. It was Christian love. I felt, every time I walked up to the church in the High Street and took part in the activities, that I really was part of the family of Collingham, accepted by all denominations and also by those who did not really belong to the church.

The Heronry

The evening quiet envelopes us around.
The trees are all full-leaved and green.
The grass is tall.
By this mound the trickling waters sound.
The geese come winging over the hill.
The ducks up-bend..the swans, stately, regal, glide on water deep and still-
Fishing for supper within reach of home
And young ones' needs. The water hens, heads bobbing to and fro-
Are busily engaged in family matters too.
The rooks swoop down – and call.
The shadows fall....
And night has come – enfolding all.

Collingham   15 Aug 1988

– 15 –
Collingham and Second Retirement?
1996

ANOTHER opportunity came to me in 1988, when I was asked if I would be willing to help at RAF Swinderby, as part of the chaplaincy team there and I agreed. I did some preliminary work helping out the chaplains with services and observing. Eventually I became the Free Church Chaplain taking a service in St Andrew's Methodist Church on the camp, at nine o'clock on a Sunday morning. There was also the Anglican Church, St Hugh's, and St Joseph's was for the Roman Catholics. I was very happy doing this work.

We went in on a Monday and worked all day taking padre's hours. These were teaching sessions because Swinderby was a training camp for new recruits. There was a set curriculum concerning such things as relationships, hygiene and discipline. Very often we had videos followed by discussion. Sometimes the discussion continued in our churches. The recruits came to Swinderby and lived there for six weeks for their training and then they 'came out' on parade. They were then drafted to other camps where they learned a trade. I was able to take the dedication services in turn with the other padres on Wednesdays. Parade services were a wonderful opportunity because mums and dads, cousins and uncles, came very proudly for the parade to watch their sons and daughters drafted out. It was a great privilege because I was allowed to take prayers in the parade, in line with the other chaplains.

We had wonderful fellowship together. It was a happy time and I enjoyed it thoroughly. Unfortunately Swinderby closed down and we all had to leave. I can remember the amazing fellowship in our St. Andrew's Church on Sunday mornings. I still keep in touch with those people who formed part of it. I often wonder what has happened to all the recruits who came through our hands. The numbers diminished as time went on and now I get a sad feeling as I go past Swinderby and see that the camp and even the runways are almost derelict. (In my imagination I can still see the flying sessions being given in little Chipmunk planes. It was a great time.)

In 1995 we felt that we had to look at our church. It needed decorating and we thought that we should refurbish it and make it more attractive. We formed 'The 95+ Committee'. We had plans to install better heating and amplification. We decided to paint the walls and to carpet the whole church. We decided to make the entrance porch more attractive by putting panes of glass in the doors. In this way people could see through to an illuminated cross and the flowers that were always there. We felt it needed a larger communion rail so that we could have a platform that could be raised. This was for the times when we had anniversaries, concerts and choirs. We took down a huge plaque which had been at the back of the pulpit and put it on one side of the church and put an illuminated cross behind the pulpit. We also hoped to change the colour of the pews by taking off the beige paint to reveal the true wood beneath. Unfortunately we found that this would be too expensive. Eventually we managed to find a paint that looked like grained wood and transformed all the paintwork. This included the pulpit and the new communion rail, which we had fitted so that it could easily be taken out. The results were really very pleasing, warm and inviting. The organ too was painted in a new warm colour. Since we carpeted under the pews as well, that, along with the new heating, made the whole much more attractive.

We had been discussing staffing in our staff meeting. Ian Wales was the minister who succeeded Richard Bielby and decided that it was time he moved out of the Newark Circuit and return to Sunderland. We would have to look around for a new minister. I had said to the staff that I thought that perhaps this would be the time for me to have a natural break and retire. The new minister could then have charge of Collingham. This was taken into account in our invitation to whoever would come to be on the staff of the Newark and Southwell Circuit.

All the procedures were put into action and in the end the Revd Richard Hooton was invited. He came to us from Ilkeston. The manse was in New Balderton, an old Victorian house. We thought it would be better for the new man to live in Collingham, since he would have charge of both Balderton and Collingham. I think some of the staff motored over along the back way and found out that it took about fifteen minutes. Richard Hooton consented to come but he was not able to move into a new manse in Collingham until the old manse in Balderton was sold.

My last service in the Collingham Methodist Church was at the end of July. That was a great occasion when we reopened the church with all its new alterations. We had a very successful flower festival in the May when we took as our theme the people who had played a part in the history of the church. It brought a lot of people onto our premises. There were all sorts of activities because we needed to raise the money for all the work we had done. There were gift services and activities in all the groups but all so happily organised. People came together as people do when they have a goal to which they are working.

This time of farewell, though it was sad, was also very happy. All kinds of people paid tribute. The Circuit gave me money gifts and my farewell service was a very memorable occasion. After the service we had a lunch and 150 people were catered for. I loved it all as, indeed, I had loved all my work. I continued to live in Collingham. I asked if the MMHA could provide me with another home. I felt that having been in Collingham as minister for 13 years and so much part of the community, it would not be easy for me to stay in Collingham. Neither would it be easy for the new man to become established. I thought that if the MMHA. could find me another place to live, it would be better if I moved out and left a clear field for Richard.

MMHA did not feel that I should move out. I was not ill. I did not need to move out on compassionate grounds. It meant that I had to look for some place that was not subsidised. I had to give three months' 'notice of termination of tenancy' and I did that. Fortunately, another supernumerary minister and his wife Pat were looking for accommodation. They came to look at my bungalow. They liked it and decided they would like to move in, so I decided to move out!

But where would I go? I was not happy to move far away from Geoff and Joan because I felt that I wanted to keep the family together. Geoff's son John, my nephew, and his wife had moved into a new house on the Brant Road, thinking that they would be near to Fred so they had moved into Lincoln before Fred, sadly, had died.

I thought that perhaps Lincoln might be a good place to live. I had ministered in the South Circuit so I came into Lincoln and began to look at properties in the North Circuit. I found a little house in Newport. I came to look at it and it seemed to be a big venture to buy. We had planned a holiday in New England in the 'Fall' and while I was away the property was sold. Maybe it was a good thing that that opportunity did go by. I contacted a friend, Maisie Richards, who I had kept in touch with since my Nottingham days. I asked her if she knew of any property in the area. Maisie quite excitedly phoned me back to say that she did know of a bungalow, which she thought might suit me. Mary Harrod had occupied it. I had known Jack Harrod from Local Preaching days. I knew that John Harrod was Jack and Mary's son and that he was a Methodist minister. He was a tutor at one of our theological colleges in Bristol. Maisie said that the bungalow Mary had occupied was empty. She had died in the July. John would possibly keep the bungalow for his own retirement so he really wanted to rent out the bungalow. This seemed right.

On 27th February 1997, I moved to 2 Carisbrooke Close, Mountfield, Lincoln. Barnes Removal vans brought all my belongings. Geoff and Joan and Margaret, Marion and David, came to help me move in and unpack. Since the bungalow had been newly decorated, the carpets were down and the curtains were up, my furniture fitted in perfectly. It was beautiful and beyond my wildest dreams. I soon felt comfortable and the place looked like home. This was to be my abode.

Marjorie's second retirement, at Collingham 1997.

– 16 –
Mountfield – Lincoln North
1997 - the present day

ON THE first Sunday of my retirement, I went to worship at Bailgate Methodist Church. I then went to register with my doctor at the Minster practice. I seemed to be surrounded by friends. Maisie Richards lives on Newport. Jean Webster, a Local Preacher, lives at 6 Carisbrooke Close. Jean and John Jacobs live at the house on the corner of Woburn Avenue. Barbara Hopkins lives at 14 Woburn Avenue. Jean and John came from Waddington where John had been a vicar. Barbara had been an Anglican deaconess. They were both retired now. In the house at the corner were Anne Newstead and William Codd who had been friends of Mary Harrod. They all had a coffee pact. They went to each other's homes at 10.30 on Monday mornings. We decided to keep the pact and we have all got to know each other.

On the corner of Carisbrooke Close there is an Abbeyfield residential home. I am a member of the house committee and also a volunteer helper. This means that I go in about once or twice a month for coffee on a Friday morning to keep in touch with the nine residents there. Every so often I take their 'fellowship' which meets on a Friday evening at six-thirty. We start with worship, have some Bible study and conclude with discussion. It is a small, close-knit family. The residents are free to come and go as they wish and their families can be in touch with them at any time They have lunch provided every day at twelve-fifteen and tea at five-fifteen. They provide food for breakfast in their own rooms. They can meet for coffee in the commonroom at ten-thirty every morning.

I have always been interested in and had an admiration for the St Barnabas Hospice. I went to see them to find out if I could help in any way. I felt that I might do training for the bereavement course. I thought that my experience in the ministry would help me in that field. They did have a kind of interview and a training session before we were allowed to work there. In my first interview I found that I would not be eligible to do any work on the wards because of my age. Apparently the insurance did not cover people of my age but I could be trained to help at the reception desk. The bereavement course cut across a lot of dates I already had so that did not seem possible at that time but I have done that course more recently. Afterwards I was asked to run a bereavement course which meets regularly and now I am one of four volunteer chaplains who attend both the Hospice and their Day Centre. I very much admire the work they do.

Freda and Nigel Ingram, who live at Thorpe on the Hill, had helped in the medieval Cathedral Library. They were there when the library was open, between May and September, for an exhibition which people came to see when they visited the cathedral. Freda and Nigel were unable to continue that work. They gave my name to Joan Goodrich, who co-ordinated the work of the volunteers there. I joined and, with another lady, I do spells when I am present at the Library to welcome visitors. Those sessions are usually in the morning from eleven until one, and in the afternoon from one-thirty to three. I enjoy that very much and I have met some very interesting people.

I wanted, if possible, to continue preaching. Terry Nowell is the Superintendent of the North Circuit. He contacted me and I said that I would like to help. He said that he thought one of the best ways of helping would be to hold communion services where they were needed. I was very glad about that. Every quarter I give so many dates to the Lincoln North Circuit. In the beginning they did ask me whether I would be running my car and if I could be responsible for being a car driver. I would be numbered on the plan to take people out to varying appointments in the Circuit. I felt that although I had kept my Mini, perhaps I was not ready to be travelling out to the country in all weathers and having the responsibility of taking and bringing back passengers. I asked if transport could be provided when I had appointments. This has been a great joy to me because I have been out to varying places in the Circuit. I have been well received and in my preparation and my preaching I really have felt that my calling has been fulfilled.

Heather and Charles provided me with a keyboard because I did not have room for my piano. I had given it away to a family in Collingham where the boy and the girl were both having piano lessons. The keyboard fulfilled my need. I am not an expert, but when I have chosen my hymns for a service, I like to play them over and make sure of the tunes. This keyboard is fun because I can press the little lever and it is an organ or a piano. There are sound effects and I can have full chords. I really have enjoyed using it.

Erica and Harry, my friends in Grimsby, said that they would lend me a computer because I had mentioned that I could take a computer course. It seems to be the modern method of communication. They brought me an Apple Mac Classic and I practised on it. Maisie belongs to a group of social workers because she trained as a nurse and worked here in Lincoln. She told me of a course that was being managed at the Boundary Social Centre. It was for disabled people in groups of ten. She and some of her former colleagues were going to take a computer course over six weeks and she asked if I would be interested. Well I was. Maisie and I went down to the course and it really was very good. The only snag for me was that the computers we used were much more up to date than the one I had at home. I found it rather difficult to officiate on my home computer when I had only to press the button on the modern computer and the printer worked as if by magic. Harry and Erica suggested that perhaps the computer ought to be updated. I had a talk with Margaret Dow who was the co-ordinator for the volunteers at Abbeyfield. She had recently purchased a word processor which, she said, filled all her needs. I thought that perhaps it would have filled mine, too. What I wanted mostly was to write out manuscripts, do my orders of service and perhaps print out copies to send to other people. Erica and Harry's son Andrew is well into computers and he said he would update mine. They brought another computer for me to keep, fixed it, and showed me how to use it.

Outside, at the back of the bungalow, it is mostly a patio but there is also a small lawn, and there is a patch of lawn at the front of the bungalow. There is a fringe of soil round the lawn at the back with a raised bed dividing it from the patio. I have had a great deal of pleasure planting new things, keeping the lawns cut and enjoying it when the sun has made it possible. Unfortunately I had a very bad fall on 14th February 1998. I did not break my hip but I sprained a lot of muscles. From then to the middle of April I could not walk very well and I was mostly dependent on transport to get me around. Margaret and Donald took me over to Willoughby for a time and my doctor was very good. Gradually I regained my confidence and could walk perfectly well again.

There is something else which gives me a sense of guilt and that is my Mini. I did bring it with me, though I did not use it very much. When I was in Collingham, especially when the RAF closed, I did not have as much need to travel. I used it to go over to Geoff and Joan's mostly, otherwise I walked. My preaching appointments were mostly in Collingham. When they were further out in the Circuit, people collected me. Erica and Harry's daughter came home from Australia and was looking for a little car. Since mine was available, I taxed and insured it and she had it. She took it home with her, had it tested and attended to and she travelled a lot in it. She went to Manchester and London and used it all the time she was at home. When it came back it was in very good condition. Since then I have not used it very much. I have been looking at the tyres and seeing if it will start up so that I can have it tested at Wright's garage here in Lincoln. Incidentally, I bought it at Wright's when I was in Hykeham. That was more than twenty years ago.

Jean Jacob, Barbara Hopkins and I have started a little study group. We are all interested in comparative religions. We thought we could do some study together, going from house to house. This we have done. We have taken the book of Hans Kuhn called *Christianity and the World Religions*. We really have enjoyed this study and our conversations around it both before and afterwards have drawn us close together.

Just before I came into Lincoln, Margaret, Donald and I had done a study course at Nottingham University in Old Testament archaeology. During the first part of my time here, I joined a WEA class in Lincoln to continue that study. After the Nottingham course we had to write a thesis. When we were on a cruise holiday this year we went to Israel. To my utter joy we went to Mount Carmel and through the Jezreel valley to lower Galilee. Our archaeology course with Nottingham University was about that area and to actually see this site was an added bonus to the holiday.

Heather and Charles, John and Val and a friend of Joan's, Geoff's wife, often come here for Joan's birthday on 31st December. It is lovely to be near enough to get the family together. Geoff and Joan came over to see me often. I go over on the bus to Skellingthorpe and I have often been to Margaret and Donald since they retired to Willoughby. The Collingham people have been absolutely marvellous. They have kept me in touch with what has been happening there and they have been to see me. We have kept our friendships alive.

Recently my brother Geoff has not been well. He had a kind

of kidney failure which, in the end, took him into hospital. He had a series of small cysts and a hernia. Then thyroid trouble was discovered and he had to have medication for that. He began to have problems with the prostate gland which meant coming and going for tests. However, after another operation, sadly Geoff died in 2002.

I am still here in 2 Carisbrooke Close and I do feel that it is my home. It is an easy place to live. I really did not need to use my car so I have let it go. The people in this little close are very friendly and neighbourly. They do not intrude but I know they would come to help, if help were needed. Burton Road Church is a small family church but a very lively church, mostly young families with small children. That is within easy walking distance. I can hear the cathedral bells and I sometimes go to the cathedral services. Shopping is easy. I can easily walk to and fro. It does seem, for the time being, that this is the place to be.

On one occasion I was asked to take a funeral. It was somebody called Downham in Mildmay Street, which is not very far away. I felt a bit apprehensive because I thought that perhaps they would not appreciate a funeral being taken by a stranger. To my surprise, when I rang the number, the son Trevor Downham said they were delighted that I was taking the funeral because I used to visit them as chaplain when he worked at Dorman Diesel's factory. Also, when they moved from this area into Lincoln, their boy, Philip, came to Swallowbeck playgroup. Then I discovered that Mr and Mrs Downham had lived in Reepham. Both of them had attended our Reepham Church. They knew my Uncle Will Maltby and my aunt, Miss Ruth Maltby, his sister, who had come to live with him when his wife died. She played the organ at the Methodist Church and so had Rhoda Downham. It was a reunion of people who had known each other. I was able to minister and take the crematorium service. The people at the crematorium also seemed glad to see me officiating again once more.

Full retirement has been a great change. I often feel guilty when I sit down with a book. I have said to myself that I must try to do some painting. I have kept up relationships with other people and I have made some new ones. Now I have felt that perhaps I should think a bit more about women in ministry and the way in which Dr Maltby fought for women to be accepted into the fulltime ministry of the church since he knew the value of the work of deaconesses. I am a product, really. He chose me, I am sure, after opposition, to be trained as a deaconess. I think I have demonstrated in my own life his choice and the fact that he believed that women in the ministry could enhance the full ministry of the Methodist Church. I have been fortunate in my ministry in being mostly on pioneer projects and working in ecumenical teams. Looking back, I am so grateful to God that I have been sent to do His work that, if I had been able to choose, I would never have felt I was capable of accomplishing. Other people have found potential in me that I never dreamed was there. It is by the grace of God and I believe by the power of his Spirit, that other people have been touched, many changed, many have grown and others have been comforted because God has used me as a tool in His service.

The Apple Tree

This year, this little apple tree
You proudly stand
Sun deckled, leaves all green,
Branches straight and strong
Bearing fruit....
Firm, luscious, heavy,
With rosy-cheeked sheen,
Some round, some long.
You proudly stand..proclaiming:
Purpose accomplished!
Harvest at hand.

A Life Enriched by
Friends and Holidays

I OUGHT to mention something about my friends. In my ministry I have had and still have very loyal friends, and because of them I have been able to do things that I would never have been able to do on my own. Much has been said about women in ministry and living alone. Some of it is true. It can be a very lonely life, though I have never found it to be so. I have always looked upon the children of the church as my 'children'. The people of the church of all ages have always been my 'family' so I have never really felt the loss of a family of my own. I did have opportunities to marry and my Mum used to say to me, "It's all right now, when you are in the prime of life and you are busy but when you get older you'll regret it, my lass, because you'll wish you had married and had a life companion and a family of your own."

Now I do begin to understand, when I am without ministry and without the authority of calling the people in the church my family and the Circuit, my colleagues and friends in the area my community. I had the right to go into homes where nobody else had. It was a tremendous privilege and people trusted me as a friend. In complete retirement life is different because I am now an ordinary person and people look upon me as such. I do understand that life could be very lonely.

One could go for a whole day and not speak to anybody because of not having the right of entry. As a result, one is perhaps slow at making advances and making friends is not as easy when one is getting older. I can see the truth in what my mother said.

I have been fortunate to have a circle of friends who have been very loyal to me. Through them I have been able to experience very good holidays and good times. Perhaps I should record some of them as a tribute to my friends.

I remember Dorothy, who taught me to drive. She was very keen on her cars. We had many a holiday exploring England: Derbyshire, the coast, Norfolk and the sea. We went to Wales, the Gower Peninsular and coastline; Scotland, I love Scotland, where we went up the east coast across to Cape Wrath and down the west coast. B and B all the time, taking risks but enjoying it.

One of my colleagues in Manchester was Susannah Neal Watson from Dublin. She was one of the deaconesses with whom I shared a house in Whalley Range. We became great friends. She felt she had to go home to Ireland and there she met the man, Norman Cook, who was to become her husband. I went over to help to marry her in our Methodist Central Hall, Dublin. I have been over to stay with her and Norman several times and we have kept in touch. Unfortunately, her husband has died and she has moved out of the family home. I have had a letter to say that she has been given a cottage and this is to become her home just outside Dublin. She has been to Madrid to stay with her sister, Grania, who went to live there with her husband some years ago. She practices as a nurse in Madrid and her husband teaches English. I count Sue as one of my treasured friends.

I met Mary Nicholson from Collingham when I was in Nottingham. I have had holidays with her because her sister, Muriel Nicholson, was one of the people I contacted first when I went to Collingham. She was ill with cancer and finally died. I knew her twin daughters, Louise and Ruth. I have kept in touch with them because I married Ruth to Mark Randall. Since their father had died Muriel gave Ruth away. That was a great celebration in Collingham because everybody knew them. Mary Nicholson and I have been up to stay with them in Aberdeen and also in York. We have also been to Swanwick together. The first weekend in June is usually a missionary weekend which Mary and I have shared. The last time we went it was the celebration of fifty years of Christianity in the United Church of South India. We had a holiday on the Isle of Wight. We were in a cottage belonging to a friend in Norfolk. We have also been on a coach trip to the Edinburgh Tattoo.

Eileen Johnson was one of the nurses in Nottingham and I kept in touch with her. Our friendship was different. She could always ring me and come and stay. I could always go and stay with her. We went to Yugoslavia. I remember the beauty of Dubrovnik, the coastal road down to Split and the clouds gathering as we travelled over to Bosnia. During the troubles in Bosnia, I remembered our travels there, especially Sarajevo and all the comings and goings of that town. We also had a holiday in Greece. We travelled through Yugoslavia to Thessaloniki and down to Athens. We went to Delphi, Athos and Corinth, where we saw the canal. We stayed on the brink of the university compound in Malta and we were there for some of the wonderful processions, celebrations and firework displays that take place there. I went to Malta again when we had a Methodist conference there. That time I was with Margaret. We stayed near Saint Julian and travelled around the island. We were in Valletta for the celebrations on St Paul's Day. I will never forget that day because of the contrast between the noisy bands and all the ticker tape coming down from the houses and the complete silence and devotion in the cathedral in Valletta.

I had known Phil in Nottingham because she had worked in one of the factories there as the 'sample' hand. She did the first make-ups of dresses that had been designed by Beth Lount. I lived with Beth Lount when I worked in the

Nottingham Mission. Phil was her right hand girl but she did not have anything to do with the church. There was another girl called Kathleen Shelton who worked alongside Phil. She was very troubled because Phil often teased her about her church affiliation. I suggested to Kath that she should invite Phil to come along to some of our social 'do's. We had an international night when we all dressed in international costume, had international songs and some international dances. Phil came along and she became interested. So much so, that she gave up her work at Hussey's factory and went to train at the National Children's Home and became a sister there. Unfortunately, her father and mother fell ill and she had to come home to nurse them. Her brother Lionel was an architect. He was not married and he travelled a lot. Phil liked to travel as well. Phil and I became friends and she was my travelling companion almost every year, for years. We went to so many places: The Isle of Man, Denmark, Spain, Gibraltar, Sardinia, Madeira, Norway, Italy, Sweden, Israel, Austria, Portugal and Jordan. We fitted in, Phil and I. I know she loved me but it was never a possessive love. She had a tremendous sense of humour and was very skilled. Phil made most of my clothes, including my ordination dress and suit. I was always well-dressed. During my time in Nottingham, I took youngsters away on holiday so I was very well equipped. I remember when I was on my first trip abroad, I was with a group of deaconesses from Liverpool. We went to the Bernese Oberland. I think the whole trip cost us £11 18s each! We stayed at the Bible College by the Lake of Thun. We travelled everywhere by train or boat. Phil had made all my dresses and the other deaconesses in our little group called me 'The Princess'.

I have always had Margaret and Donald since my Manchester days, when Margaret was a nurse and Donald a medical student. When I came to Lincoln, I found that they were in practice there. I have been privileged to join them on many holidays. There were short breaks with Margaret, of two or three days, in Yorkshire and Holland. There were longer holidays too in Crete and Turkey, where we visited the seven churches. We went to Canada, Sri Lanka, France, Northumberland, the National Parks of the USA, Cyprus, New England, and in 1998 we went on a cruise round the Mediterranean. It was a lecture cruise starting at Izmir and going to Ephesus, Syria, Lebanon, Cyprus, Israel, Egypt and Jordan. We saw the Pyramids and the Valley of the Kings. We sailed down the Suez Canal, crossed Sinai and visited Petra. A tremendous holiday! It was the holiday of a lifetime and full of experiences. We saw places I have always wanted to visit. We were able to visit from on board ship, after having lectures telling us about the places that we were going to see. All the visits were in well-organised groups and it was lovely to come back to the ship to relax with friends. It was a wonderful experience. Margaret sent me a parcel of photographs. They are copies of the ones she took on this holiday. I took days looking through them and reliving those times again. I have always been grateful to Margaret and Donald for sharing their family with me. I was invited to Peter's wedding. We have been to see Richard, another of their sons, and Jill, their daughter, and their grandson James. They have allowed me to feel that I was part of their family.

Liz and Charles are in Manchester. I knew them in Manchester and I have kept in touch with them ever since. They have invited me to stay with them and they have been to stay with me. I have been privileged to keep in touch with their girls, Pamela and Jill, and now with their families too.

I have also kept in touch with Celia and Frank Offiler in Nottingham. They have always sent me the Nottingham Mission magazine. I have been to see them and they have been to see me. I have also kept in touch with June. She was a girl I got to know in hospital. Her home was in Cricklade and now she is in Hove, Brighton. I count her and her husband among my friends. June Wright was a girl I knew in Nottingham. She got married and had a family and now she lives in Kensington, London. It is good to have friends who have different personalities and with whom one has different activities and share different interests.

There was a girl called Hetty who came to Hykeham when I was the minister there. She had been an officer in the Salvation Army. She became a member of the Methodist Church. When she went to live in Shepherd's Bush in London she joined the River Court Methodist Church. She was the organist there and was very happy until they became part of another grouping with the URC. This was formed by the amalgamation of the Congregational and Presbyterian Churches. She always missed the liturgy of the Methodist Church.

She would sometimes ring me on a Sunday night and say, "Have you taken communion today?" I would say, "Yes". "Did you use the book?" "Yes, I always use it because I am proud of the Methodist liturgy." And she would say, "I wish we could, you know, it's always so sloppy our communion service. It is neither one thing nor the other!"

I kept in touch with Hetty until she died in one of our Methodist homes. The chaplain there looked after her. I also kept in touch with Rene, who lives in Louth now. She was one of the people I vaguely remember from when I was very young. We keep in touch mainly because of our association in a farming community then. There are many people like that such as Maisie. I knew her in Nottingham but I also knew her mother here, in Lincoln, so we were bound together by our associations.

We realise, don't we, at Christmas time how many of our friends have gone. When we are getting older, gaps appear in our relationships but we remember our friends. I am grateful for the way my friends have enhanced thought, life, activity and love. Receiving the warmth of love and loyalty through the years has wonderfully enriched my life.

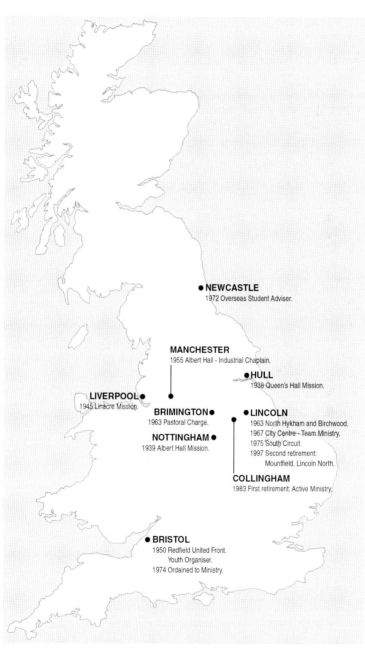

● **NEWCASTLE**
1972 Overseas Student Adviser.

MANCHESTER
1955 Albert Hall - Industrial Chaplain.

●**HULL**
1938 Queen's Hall Mission.

LIVERPOOL●
1945 Linacre Mission.

BRIMINGTON●
1963 Pastoral Charge.

●**LINCOLN**
1963 North Hykham and Birchwood.
1967 City Centre - Team Ministry.
1975 South Circuit.
1997 Second retirement:
        Mountfield, Lincoln North.

NOTTINGHAM ●
1939 Albert Hall Mission.

COLLINGHAM
1983 First retirement: Active Ministry.

● **BRISTOL**
1950 Redfield United Front.
        Youth Organiser.
1974 Ordained to Ministry.

Where Marjorie served in her ministry.

Harvest

Combines reap the harvest now.
The grain brought in by truck.
The straw is burned in long straight lines
And covered o'er with muck.
There's dust and dirt and noise and haste.

No poetry now.
Not to my taste.

No fragrant smell. No quiet sound.
No slow, deep rhythm.
No sheaves are bound.
No gleaning over the stubbled field.
No sampling of the ripe corn yield.
No neat tall stacks.
No final load
With celebrations on the road.
No buttered buns and strong sweet tea
Eaten with laughter, welcomed with glee.
No harvest supper with kith and kin.

Just......

Well, that's it – The harvest's in.